How Still the Riddle

Also By
Francine Marie Tolf

The Rough Edge of Joy
Joliet in My Blood
Eighteen Poems to God and a Poem to Satan
Shadow Town
Prodigal
Rain, Lilies, Luck
Joliet Girl
Windy City Fragments
Like Saul
Blue-flowered Sundress

How Still the Riddle

POEMS BY

FRANCINE MARIE TOLF

ART BY GALE TOLF

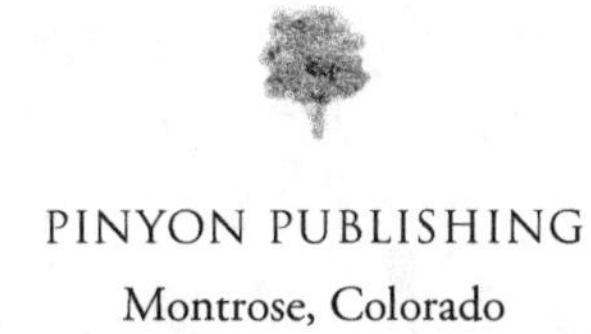

PINYON PUBLISHING
Montrose, Colorado

Cover Art by Gale Tolf

Photograph of Gale Tolf by Marcy Darin

Design by Susan Entsminger

First Edition: December 2017

Pinyon Publishing
23847 V66 Trail, Montrose, CO 81403
www.pinyon-publishing.com

Library of Congress Control Number: 2017960591
ISBN: 978-1-936671-48-9

ACKNOWLEDGMENTS

The Lyric: Allegra's Song, Fireflies, I Have Known Moments, Lines for a Rainy Night, The Night Tree

Pinyon Review: The Cottonwood Tree, Francis: Two Legends, Iris, The Island of Discussion, Late Summer Gold, Sonnet for a Sister, Summer Night, Listening to Debussy

"Marigolds in November" and "Summer Night, Listening to Debussy" were awarded Works of Merit by the Northwoods Art and Books Festival.

"Late Summer Gold" was awarded the Popular Choice by the Northwoods Art and Books Festival.

"Lines for a Rainy Night" was awarded First Place by *The Lyric*'s annual Student Poetry Contest.

Contents

Preface 1

Come In, Come In 5
Late Summer Gold 6
The Leopard Lily 7
The Desert Father 9
I Have Known Moments 12
Big Wind 13
At the Fountain of Joy 14
The Night Tree 16
Francis: Two Legends 17
Song 20
Clee, the Fearsome Siamese 21
Sonnet for a Sister (who was once my best friend) 23
Moon 24
Iris 26
Allegra's Song 27
Five Mushrooms at the Base of a Birch Tree 29
Spring Sniffed 30
Sing Me a Poem 32
Judas 34
Marigolds in November 35
One Day 36
Sheeba, Cat of Cats 39
Lines for a Rainy Night 40
My Secret 41

The Hermit 45
When Misha Sleeps 46
Claire Playing Brahms 47
The Private, Quiet Dreams 50
Fireflies 51
Seals 52
White Horse in Green Dusk 55
The Island of Discussion 58
Fragment 59
The Wild Beasts 60
Goblin Fruit 61
Happiness 62
Lillybird, the Enlightened Cat 63
Children of the Day 64
Summer Night, Listening to Debussy 66
"How Still the Riddle Lies" 67
This Night's a Witch 69
After Reading the Book of Job 70
The Cottonwood Tree 71
The Moon-Flower 75
All Living Things 77
Farewell 81

About the Author 84
About the Artist 85

PREFACE

My mother loved the rhyming poems I wrote in college. They were the first poems I wrote as an adult, and she acted as if reading my fledgling sonnets and ballads were a privilege rather than a favor. Mom not only loved me, she believed in me. From the autumn day in 1977 when I wrote my first poem ("Marigolds in November," which is part of this collection) until I graduated from Joliet, Illinois' very own College of Saint Francis in 1980, I shared just about every poem I wrote with her.

Writing was everything to me. Yet a few years after graduating, I stopped. I didn't take it up again seriously until many years later, strangely enough just weeks after my mother died. I had a lot of catching up to do. I worked hard at my craft for thirteen years and finally published a full-length poetry collection in 2010. I was fifty-two years old. Mom never got to read that book, or any of the poetry books I have since published.

She won't get to read this one either, but I think *How Still the Riddle* might have been her favorite. She loved rhythm and sound and musicality, and I tried to instill these elements in each poem in this collection. It's the lyrical fruit of a lifetime; I wrote some of these poems at nineteen, and some at fifty-eight. (And here's something that may surprise you: if certain poems are tinged with sadness, they were probably written when I was twenty, not fifty.)

The art in *How Still the Riddle* was created by my late sister, Gale Tolf. The pictures do not correspond specifically with any of the poems, but I knew Gale's ink and watercolor drawings, inspired by myth, legend, and fairytale, would complement them perfectly. Gale would have been delighted to be part of this book. She was so proud of my accomplishments as a writer. She was a poet herself, and a wise and generous woman with a wicked sense of humor.

I would like to think Gale and Mom were with me in spirit as I put together this collection. They didn't mind that I had the audacity to invoke William Blake in the first and last poem. Blake didn't mind either!

He knew I wasn't putting myself in his company (although the William Blake that I know wouldn't mind) but honoring the light and darkness, the mystery and wisdom of *Songs of Innocence and of Experience*.

There's light and darkness in this collection too. Some of the poems are appropriate to read out loud to children. Some are for more mature readers. You'll recognize which poems are for "children young" and which are for "children old."

It's my deep and sincere wish that you'll enjoy reading all of them.

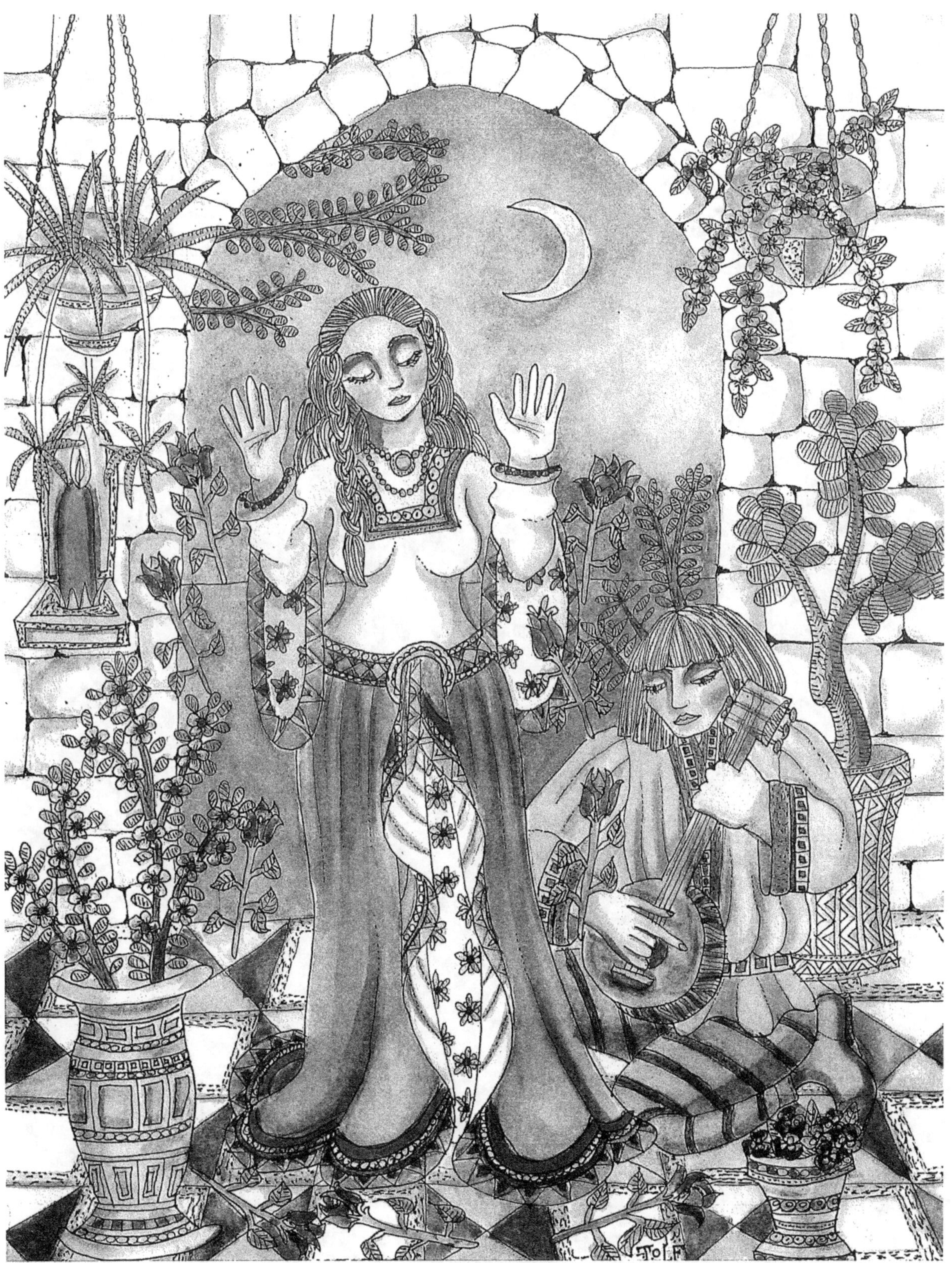

COME IN, COME IN

My golden hair is turning gray,
my sins are sinned, my wild oats flung.
Now's the time to pen a book
of rhymes for children old and young.

I've wrinkles, but my joy's awake!
Thank God for every song that's sung
by crickets, snakes and prairie dogs
and all God's children, old and young.

Blake saw angels draped in trees
where ripened pears and apples hung.
Dear poet, bless this humble book
of rhymes for children old and young.

LATE SUMMER GOLD

Luxuriant and lush, late summer
mornings melt like easy gold
to full-ripe afternoons, so humming-
rich a heart can barely hold
such heavy wealth.
                                        I tell myself
to savor slow the molten skies
and locusts' lazy buzz-saw chants
and laden trees and dragon flies—
but never do.
                                Day slips by dusk
and leaf by tree, and moon by sun,
till all the gold I had a while—
but squandered like a fool—
                                                is gone.

THE LEOPARD LILY

A leopard lily burns bright orange
in gardens pink with hollyhocks
and yellow daisies, purple phlox—
a leopard lily burns bright orange.

Her pistil like a scepter springs
from crown-like petals arching back,
oh crown-like petals speckled black.
Her pistil like a scepter springs.

Don't dare to touch its velvet tip.
This lily's fierce; she knew from birth
that only wild things sing her worth.
She gives them honeyed dew to sip.
Don't dare to touch her velvet tip.

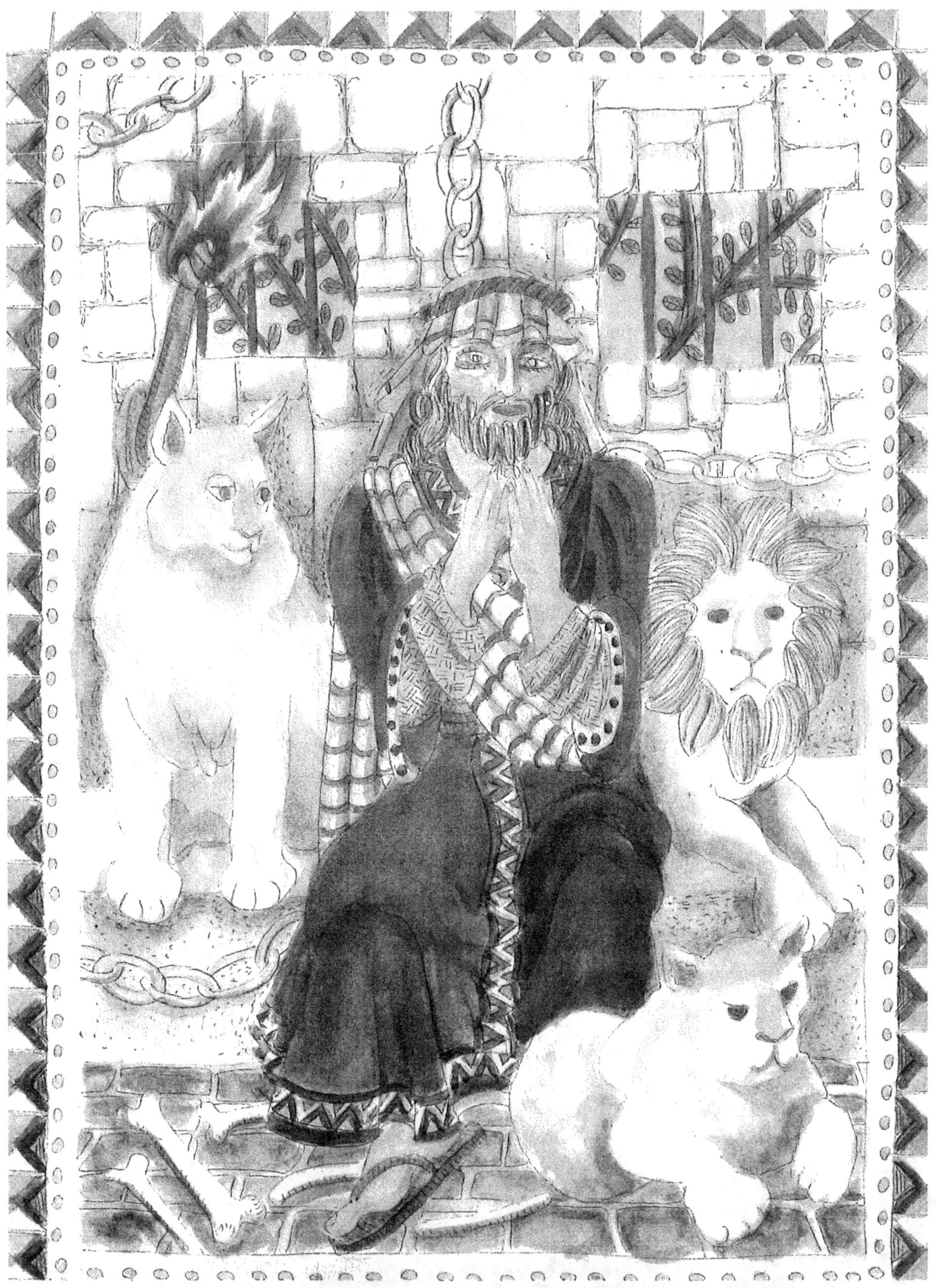

THE DESERT FATHER

Because he sought to cleanse his worldly soul
from stains of twisted truths his city taught,
and all the worthless pleasures sold and bought
by desperate people craving to be whole,

He left the home and comforts he possessed,
and took his sins away to desert sands,
and there did fast and pray in barren lands,
and might have lived a holy man and blessed;

For though by many visions he was tried,
he wasn't prey to any but the last:
reflecting on temptations he had passed,
he stumbled on the cunning sin of pride.

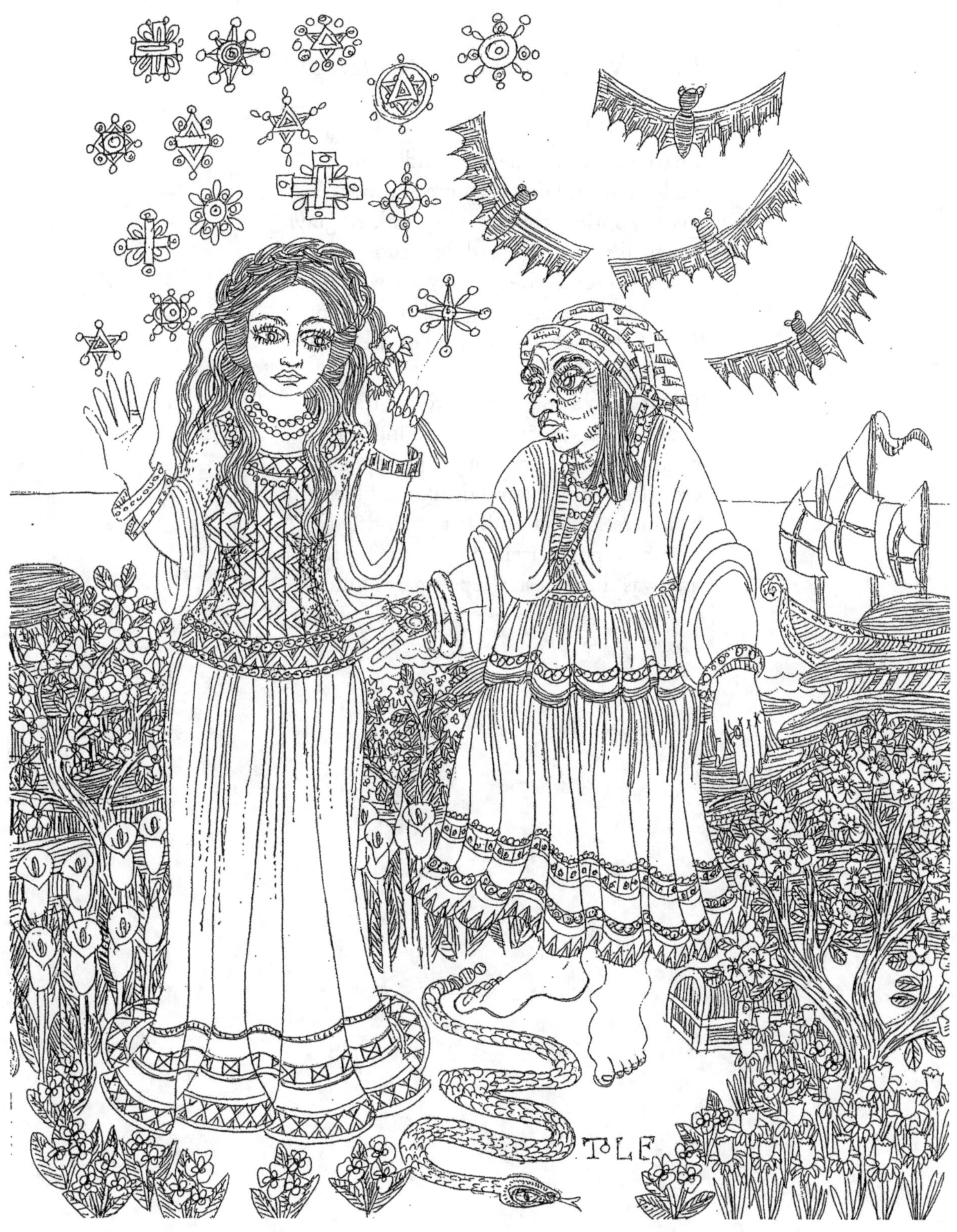

I HAVE KNOWN MOMENTS

I have known moments, standing in the blue
of dusk, or walking on a moist brown day
in early spring, the water sky washed gray,
when all that I regretted, longed to do
was lifted for a while: I only knew
a peace embracing earth and air and sky.
And then it seemed the core of me was joy.

But at a day's end, seeing from a train
gray factories against malingering light,
or in the smoke and laughter of a night
crowded with talk and drinking, I have known
a sadness so profound, felt so alone,
it seemed grief surfaced from the heart of me
and was the stillest, deepest part of me.

BIG WIND

Big wind that ripped the leaves off trees
and flung them at the sky to race
in giddy rings, rebuffed my tears,
dashing them cold against my face.

And that was good—I knew it then—
was glad for the raw, rain-soaked air
and ragged clouds that traveled low
and soaring wind that whipped my hair

in tangles. Pain dissolved in something
greater there, and if I cried,
I cried for something wild and harsh
and timeless—not the hurt inside.

AT THE FOUNTAIN OF JOY

Sienna

In yellow dusk, the pigeons of this square
wait patiently to sip and bathe and preen.
The fountain where they meet is named for joy.
These birds are joyful, too—purple and green,
their shining breasts, mellifluous their coos!
They trust they are as beautiful as swans.
And wait their turn to bathe in golden bliss
as yellow evening deepens into bronze.

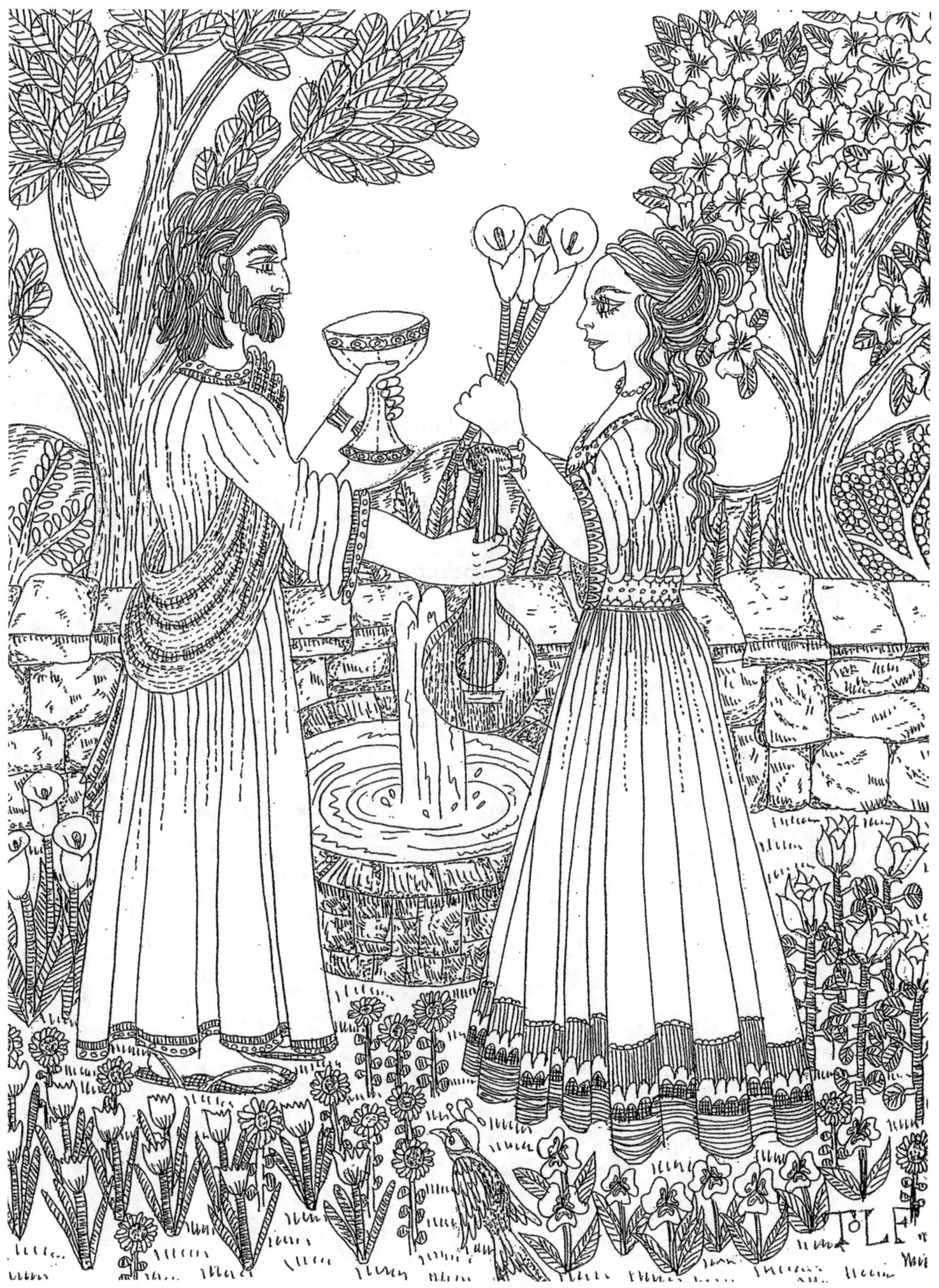

THE NIGHT TREE

I know a tree of snarled wood
whose bark is eaten smooth as bone;
a twisted crone,
ensnaring stars in gnarled wood
at nighttime when I walk alone,
at night, alone.

And always underneath I linger,
caught in some nocturnal spell;
the tree knows well,
and beckons with one crooked finger
gloatingly, as if to tell
a secret hidden from the sun—
but I pass on.

FRANCIS: TWO LEGENDS

Some moments sing and always will,
transcending time to timelessness.
A small man dances on a hill
at sunset, bowing low to bless

wildflowers dancing at his feet.
Moon's on his shoulder, sky's ablaze!
This poet's blood thrills to the beat
of earth and heaven breathing praise.

Some moments transcend even song.
Francis and a leper meet.
The monk, repulsed, attempts to fling
a few coins at the sick man's feet.

Then Francis looks into his eyes
and light breaks through the mortal plain
and shatters inequalities.
A sea of wonder, joy and shame

roars through him as he runs to hold
the filthy man, and kiss his face.
Past fear and hate, inside a field
of fragrant love, the two embrace.

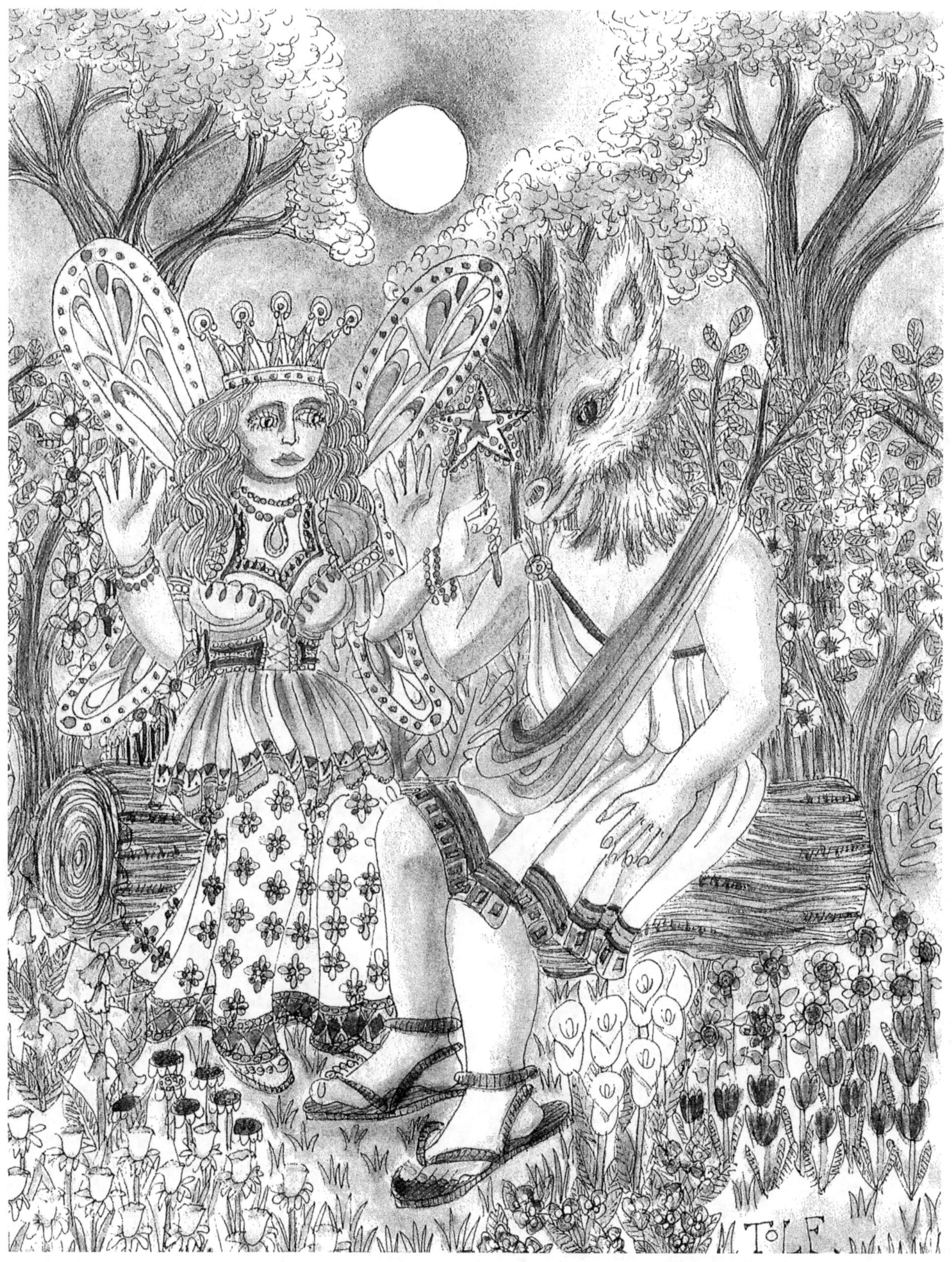
M. T°L F.

SONG

Gold ring, silver dish,
weave a rhyme, bury a wish.
In twenty years, the watered plot
may yield a blue forget-me-not.

Owl's wood, eagle's nest,
my true love's neither east nor west.
What loves I have live in my head.
(I deal in words, not flesh and blood.)

Wolf's fang, tiger's claws,
does loneliness have gaping jaws?
Some days I've felt them yawn so wide
I'd swear a world could fit inside.

CLEE, THE FEARSOME SIAMESE

No stealthy tiger slinking prey could be
as stealthy or as resolute as Clee.
Disdaining legion threats that lurk
beneath the chair—
behind the door!—
he stalks the house in fearless dignity.

For he's a long-legged, tawny Siamese.
A royal cat! who walks with princely ease
through tiger lily jungles where
he swats at flies
with flashing eyes
of china blue, and fiercely chases leaves.

The dashing poodles Barnaby and Moe
are arrogantly scorned by him, although
when no one sees, a slim brown paw
will jab with glee
at Barnaby
or tickle Moe's soft ear, or pluck his toe.

But Beauregard, the silent, lumbering tom
who lost an ear on some nocturnal roam
and has no use for dignity,
frivolity,
or royalty,
is held in great respect by Clee—and left alone.

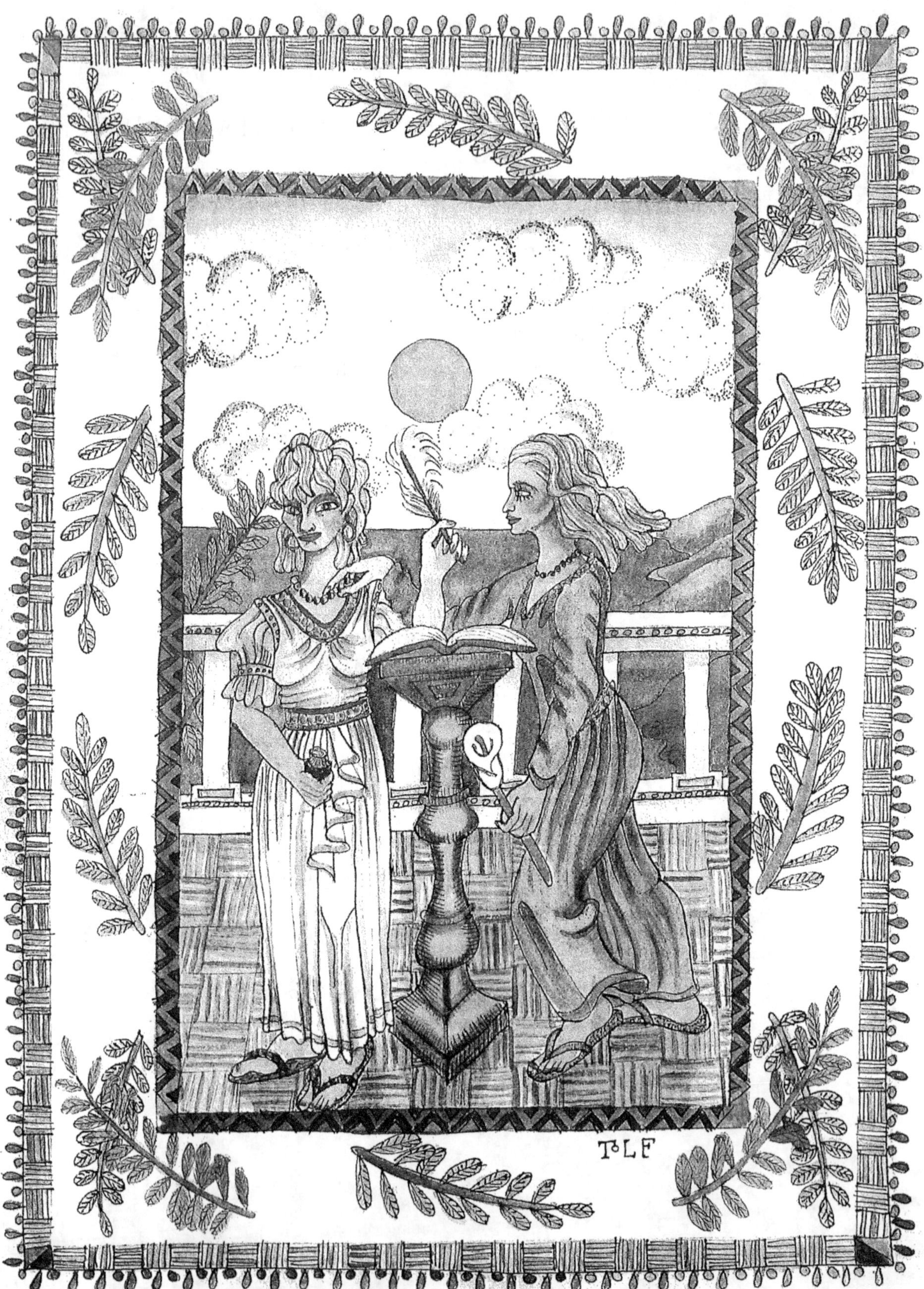
T.L.F

SONNET FOR A SISTER (WHO WAS ONCE MY BEST FRIEND)

The final winter you and I were home,
what walks we took! Past the cathedral, past
bare field and highway, striding hard and fast
as the orange sun sank low. Our talk would roam
from small to large—the way the crisp wind combed
snow into sand dunes; whether true love lasts—
while boots scrunched ice, and trees and houses cast
blue shade on white. How it all seems a poem
now, stilled and true, the sun forever sinking
behind bare trees, the west forever stained
fresh gold and rose, and one pale diamond blinking.
What if it's gone? It was there once, and you
and I, our rare, deep closeness, left ingrained
a radiance. May it quicken your heart, too.

MOON

That is no mass of lunar stone—
it's far too insubstantial.
Impossible that men have trod
that beaten, silver shell!

Why, anyone of sense can see
a giant with a roving eye
lumbered onto craggy cliff
and plucked it from the diamond sky.

Descending into mountain cave,
he hammered it till paper-thin
with magic anvil luminous—
and then he hung it back again.

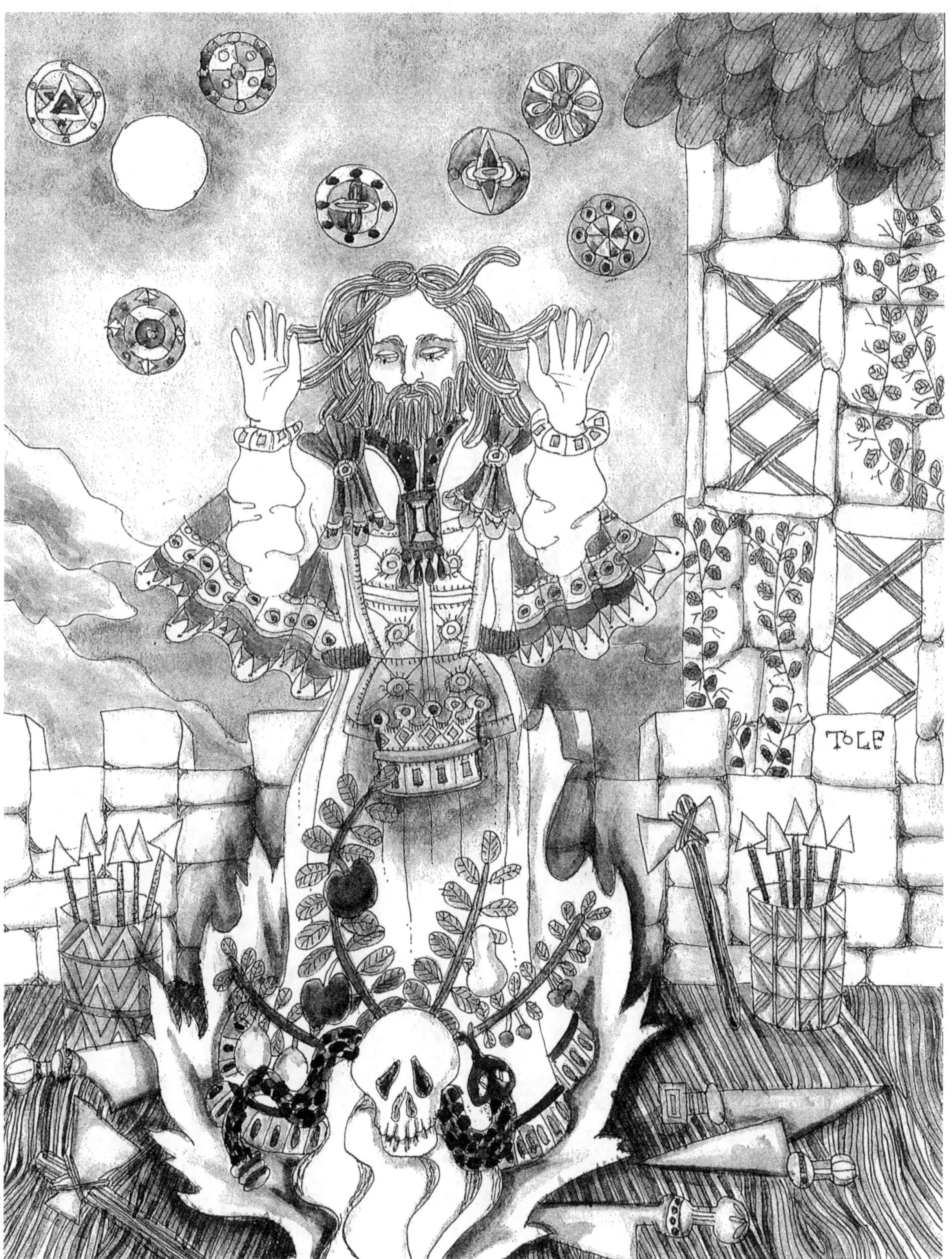
TOLE

IRIS

Her petals drip like trembling tears
that do not spill; richer than sky,
their purple-blue. Distilled in her
is summer's depth and beauty's sigh.

ALLEGRA'S SONG

I took my love for him to where the sky
is ringed with gulls come shoreward from the sea,
thinking the Northern solitude would free
my longing, let my love fade soft and die,
as even strong love wrapped in grayness will.
But every arcing seabird's desolate cry
became my own and sobbed I loved him still.

On a stormy sea rock, windy water black,
waves swirling white, the slender cliffs behind,
I tried to fling my sore love to the wind
that wildly keened—wind, laughing, flung it back.
No storm could shake the hurting from my breast,
nor calm—for when in still dusk I would walk,
I saw his face upon the burnished west.

At last, longing for peace and nothing more
one numbing day, a hard white sky above,
I buried all my secret, hurting love
deep in the cold sand of that Northern shore.
Nor can I fathom whether it beats still
beneath the winter's sleet and ocean's roar—
having no heart to ache in me and tell.

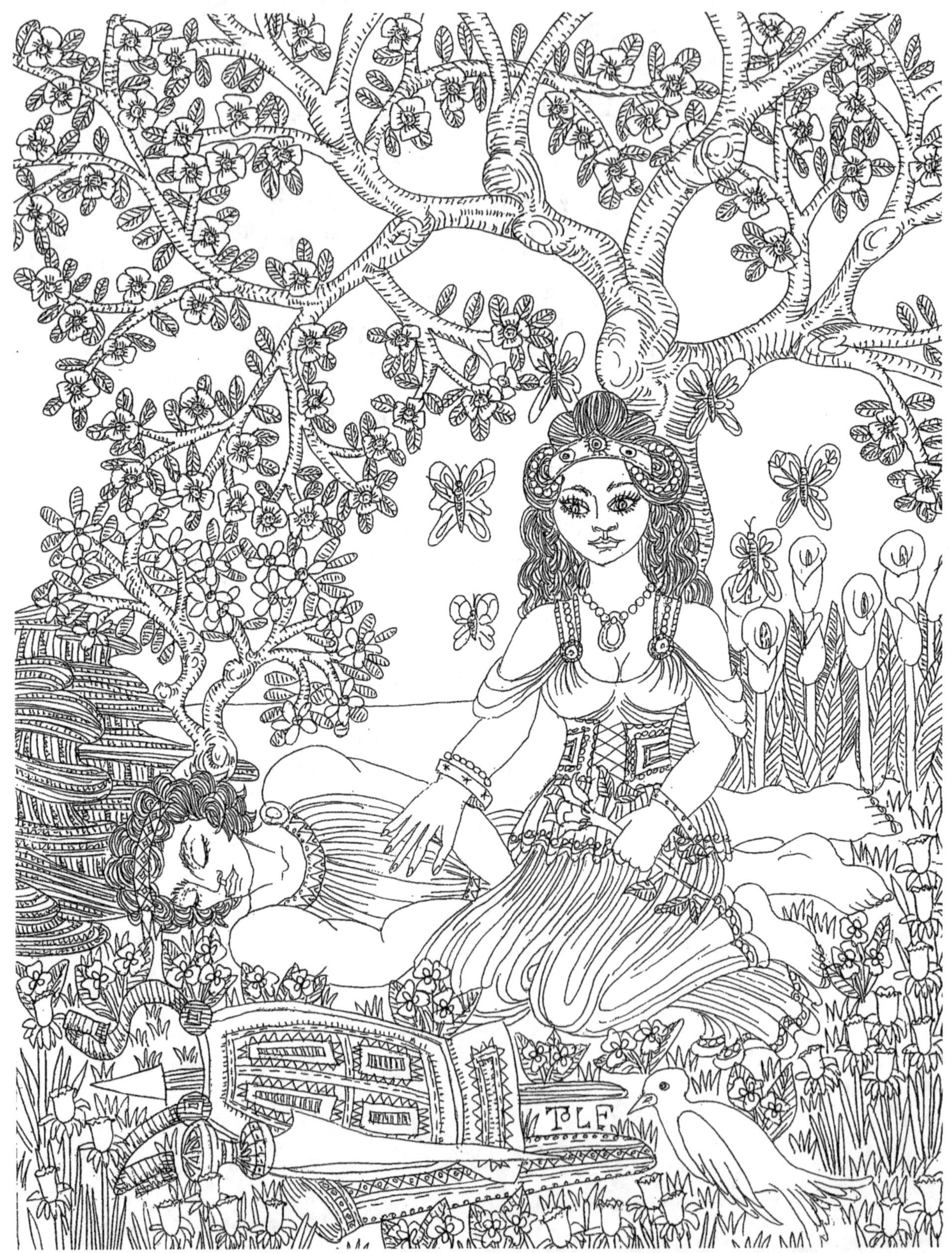
TLF

FIVE MUSHROOMS AT THE BASE OF A BIRCH TREE

In a kingdom cool and dark and moist,
they heave and push through soggy loam,
not knowing why they strain to leave
this rich delight:
                                        then burst full-grown
into the light—pale, fleshy knobs,
guileless as lambs, blind to the day.
I bend to touch one cool white bulb—
ah, tenderly!—
                                            and walk away.

SPRING SNIFFED

On a day
when there's a bud
and mottled snow
on puddled mud,

A chilled blue sky
that's cirrus-swirled
with marble white,
all twirled and whirled,

Arranging and changing
from elegant fluff
to slumbering dragons
and magical stuff,

Every *if*
becomes a *when*
and dormant dreams
awake again.

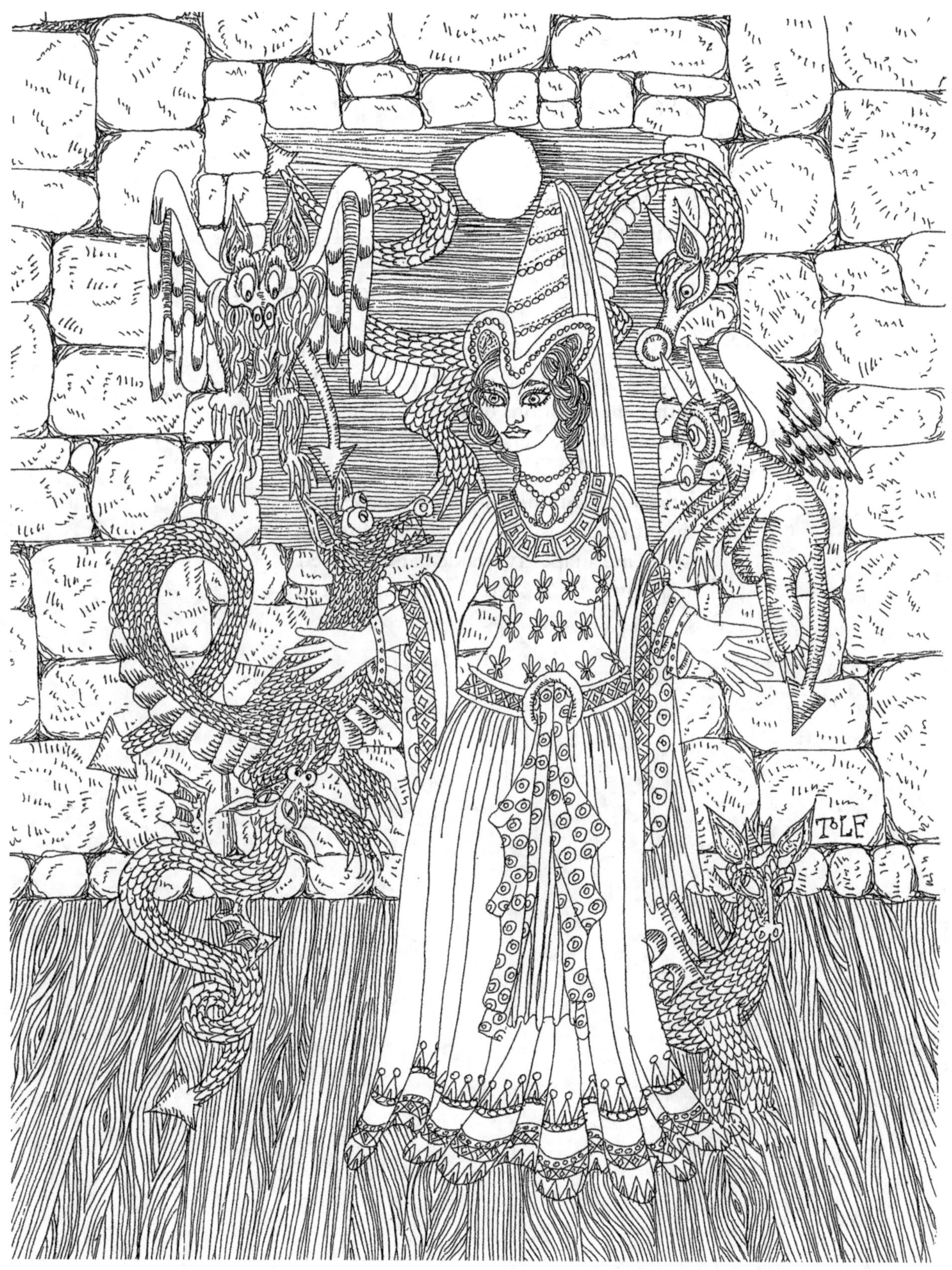

SING ME A POEM

Sing me a poem to untangle the snarls
of circumstance knit into puzzles each day;
unravel the enigmas knotted in gnarls
and snip off the loose ends and throw them away!

Tell me a tale to unearth the great mysteries
studied by sages and wizards of old;
gather the questions of all human history,
spin me the answers in scarlet and gold.

Unriddle the riddles and after you've mended
the tattered illusions and patches and shreds,
weave me a tapestry braided and blended
and woven from poetry's magical threads.

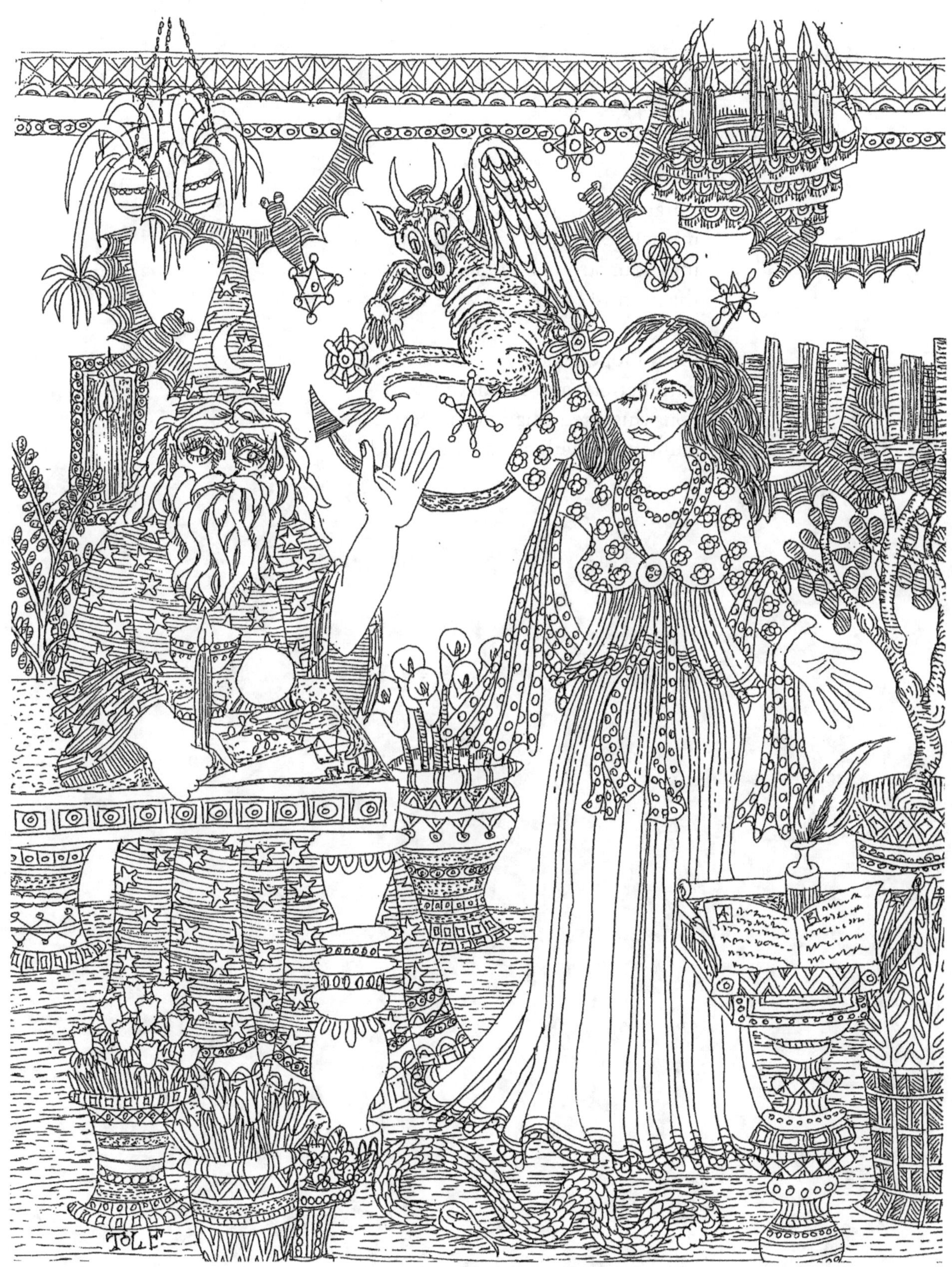

JUDAS

Enraptured hour when you drew
me helpless, joyous, still unsure
into your strong embrace and swore
the promises you gave were true.

Then Hope, when you had stroked my soul
with flattery, and I believed,
you whispered I had been deceived—
and left me with a mocking smile.

MARIGOLDS IN NOVEMBER

What thief who sucked the colors out of leaves,
and spat them brown and curling to the breeze,
and hid the sun behind a sheet of gray,
mysteriously permitted you to stay?

A hundred suns that tremble in the cold,
and shake their spangled globes of ruffled gold,
tumbling over broken stems they lean
to touch the spidery hands of evergreen.

The final sparks of autumn's dying fire
are tangled in a twisted snarl of briar,
and though it's true a bitter season reigns,
this prayer, this steadfast song of joy, remains.

ONE DAY

One day I will write poems, lovely poems.
They will be the mirror of my soul,
clean and whole,
saying precisely what I want to say,
and inspiration will not run away
from a white sheet of paper that holds it at bay.

My words will fall like raindrops in the autumn rain,
caught on measured lines of red and blue—
a lyrical clue
to thoughts and dreams that ache to be expressed:
elusive jewels hidden in a treasure chest
that vanish then appear, as would an uninvited guest.

My home will be a cabin near the open sea.
On a shore where mystery meets time,
each day I'll climb
up rocky cliffs etched tall against an endless sky.
Each night the sea will sing her lullaby—
the moon, the stars, perhaps some seals, and I.

I'll have dug the truth out from a thousand lies
wrapped in subtle layers of fear and hate.
I'll contemplate
the waves, and God, and what it means to be,
while seagulls dip and balance over sea.
I'll read of mystic lands and lore and write my poetry.

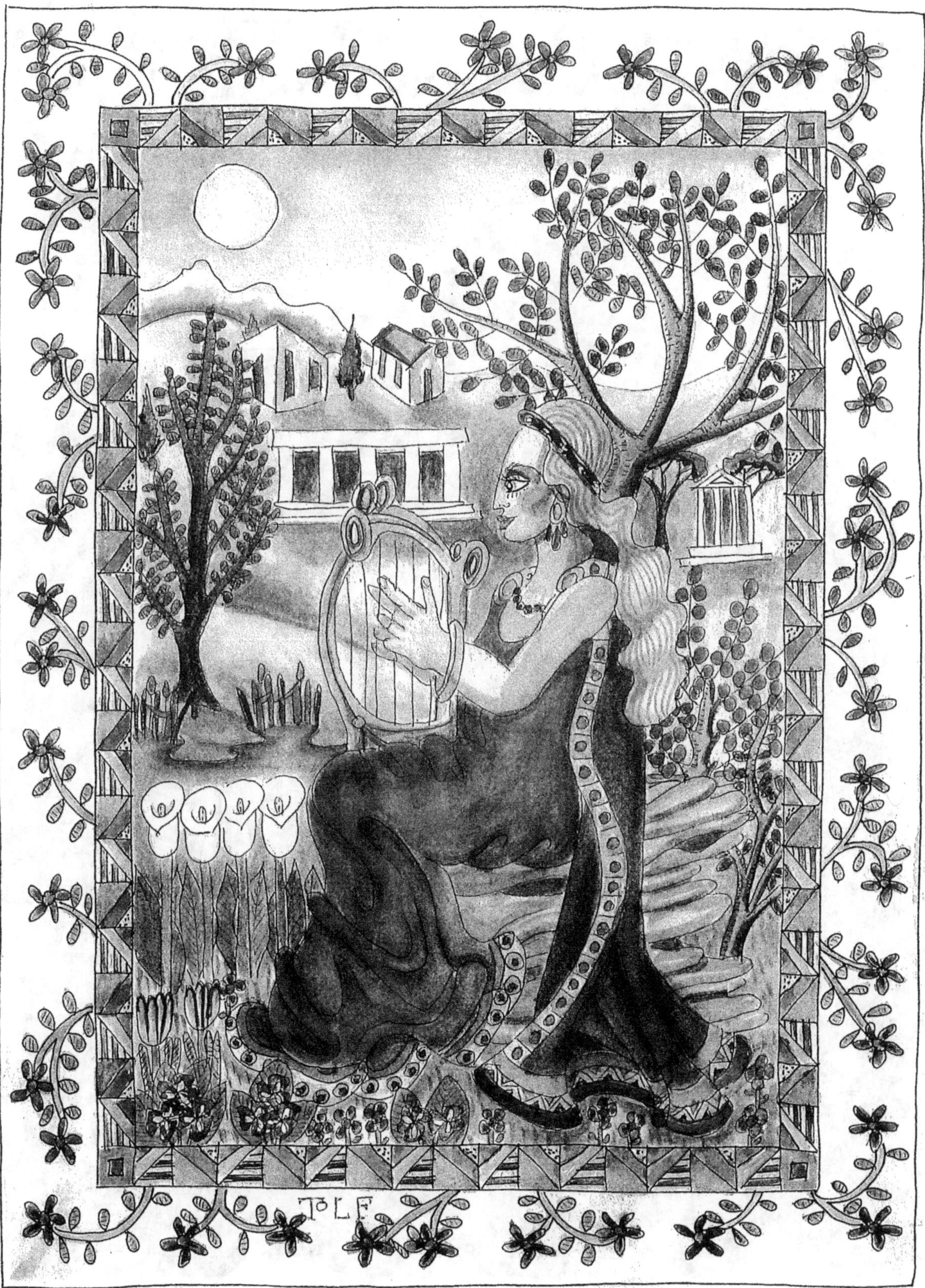

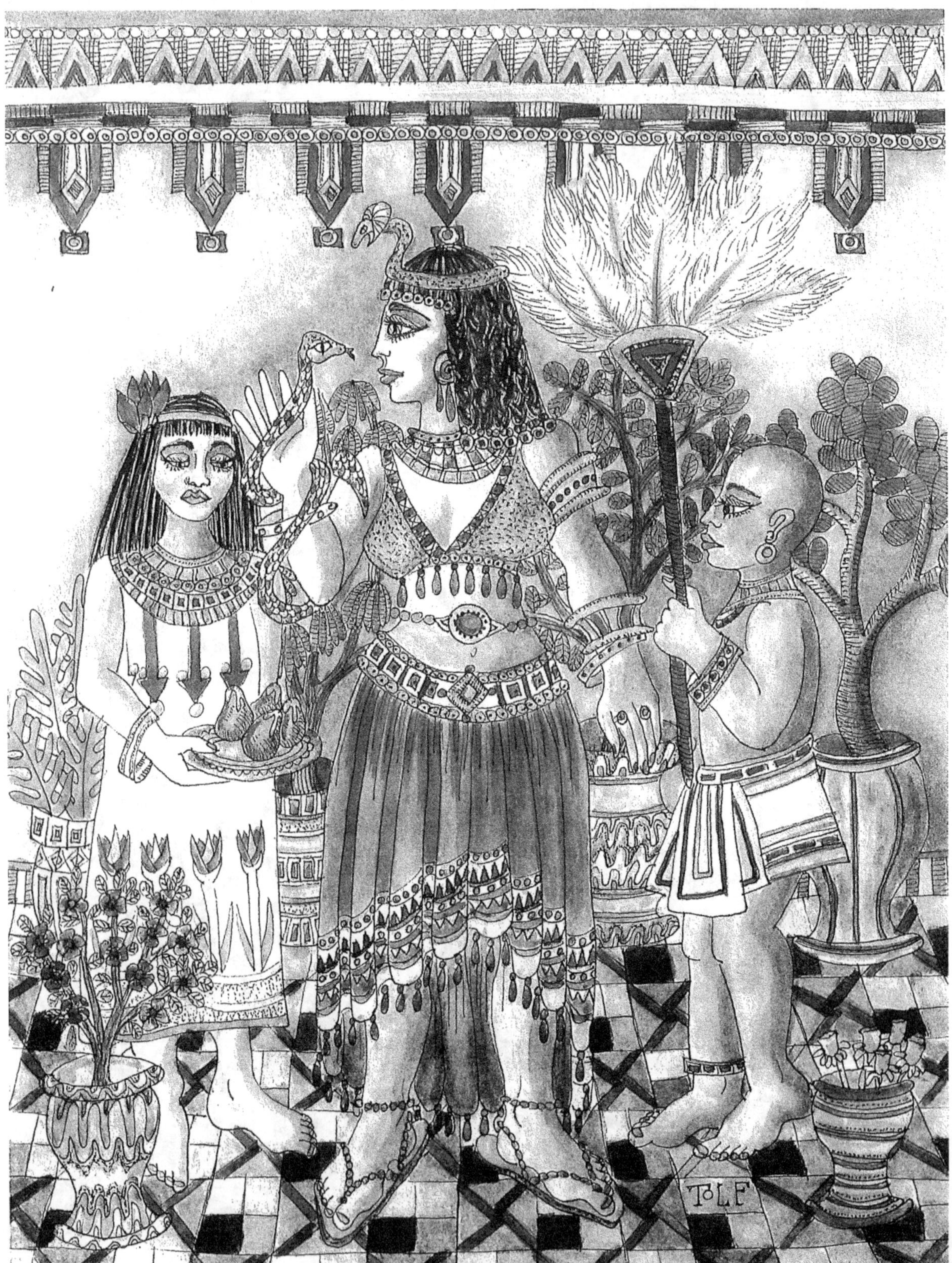
ToLF

SHEEBA, CAT OF CATS

I named my black cat Sheeba,
but call her lots of things:
Shabina, Beana, Lamb and Bean,
Young Miss and Babykins and Queen.
A lesser cat might be confused
by all the silly names I use,
but *Sheeba* knows she's Cat of Cats,
and that is that.

She has green eyes, my Sheeba,
and royal whiskers white.
Her ears are tall, her tail is proud,
her toes are clean, her purr is loud.
A cat of lesser character
might preen and boast and brag. Not her!
She knows she's Sheeba, Cat of Cats,
and that is that.

LINES FOR A RAINY NIGHT

Come walk in me a while. Leave behind
your lighted rooms for dark and gleaming streets,
and let them take you where they will. Drink deep
the fresh, clean gusts of night rain mixed with wind,
and hear low waters rush beneath your feet.

See how thin raindrops dance in streetlamp's light
and cling to slender branches; hear the cry
of a lone foghorn sobbing to the sky
and feel its desolation; be the flight
of distant trains, become a dark wind's sigh.

For now there's neither eye nor voice nor sun
to question what you are, or feel, or see.
In kindness, I grant anonymity,
a gift no dawn can ever give. So come
and know some peace a while, be part of me.

MY SECRET

There is no one to cry my secret to.
A deaf wind whispers, *Even if there were,*
your lover could not share it if he knew.
He could not pierce the secret to its core
and share it with you even if he knew.

No matter if in all else we were one,
and shed, for love, all camouflage and art,
locked far away, locked deep in blood and bone,
the deepest of myself would lie apart;
the deepest of myself would be alone.

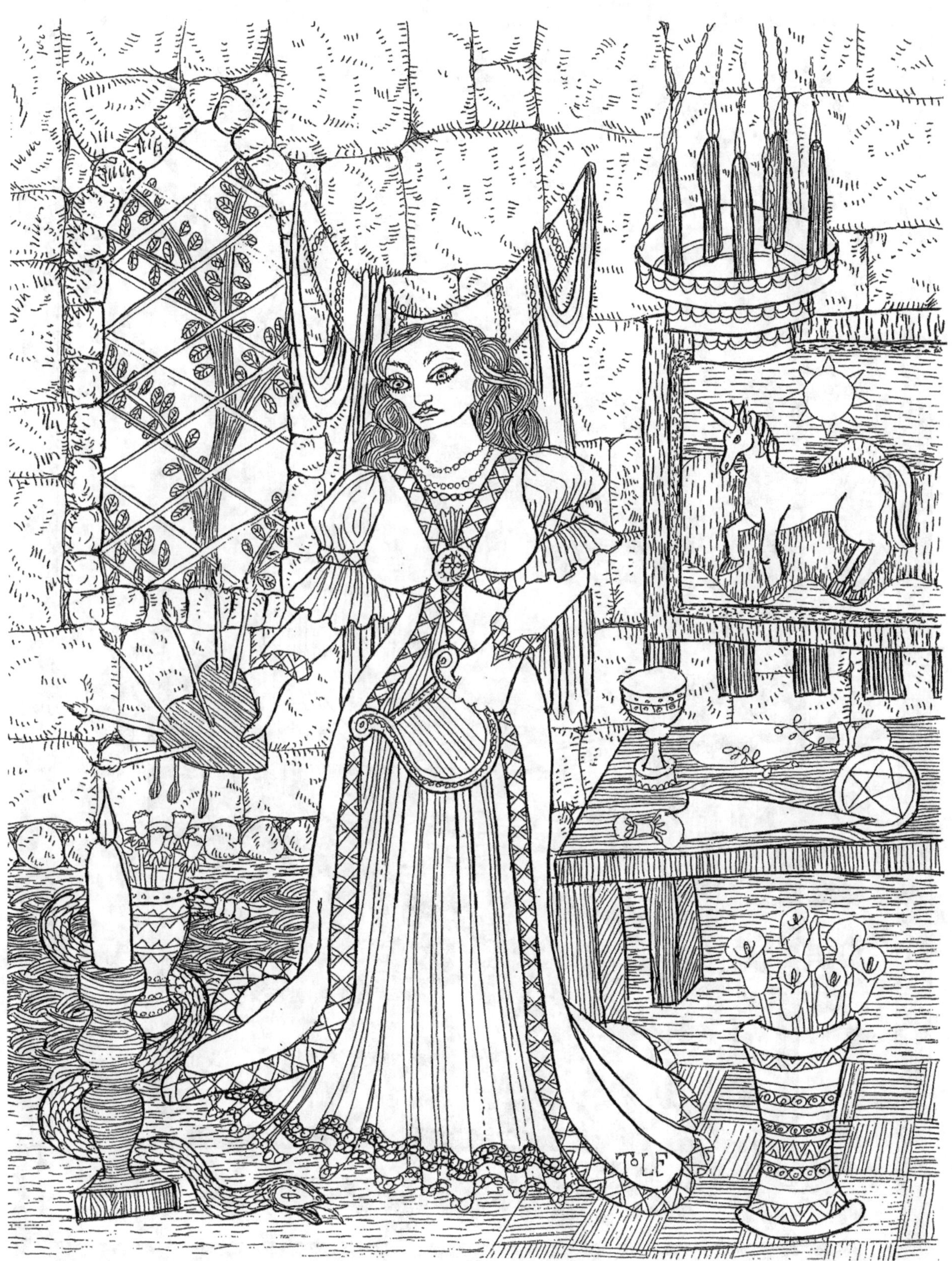

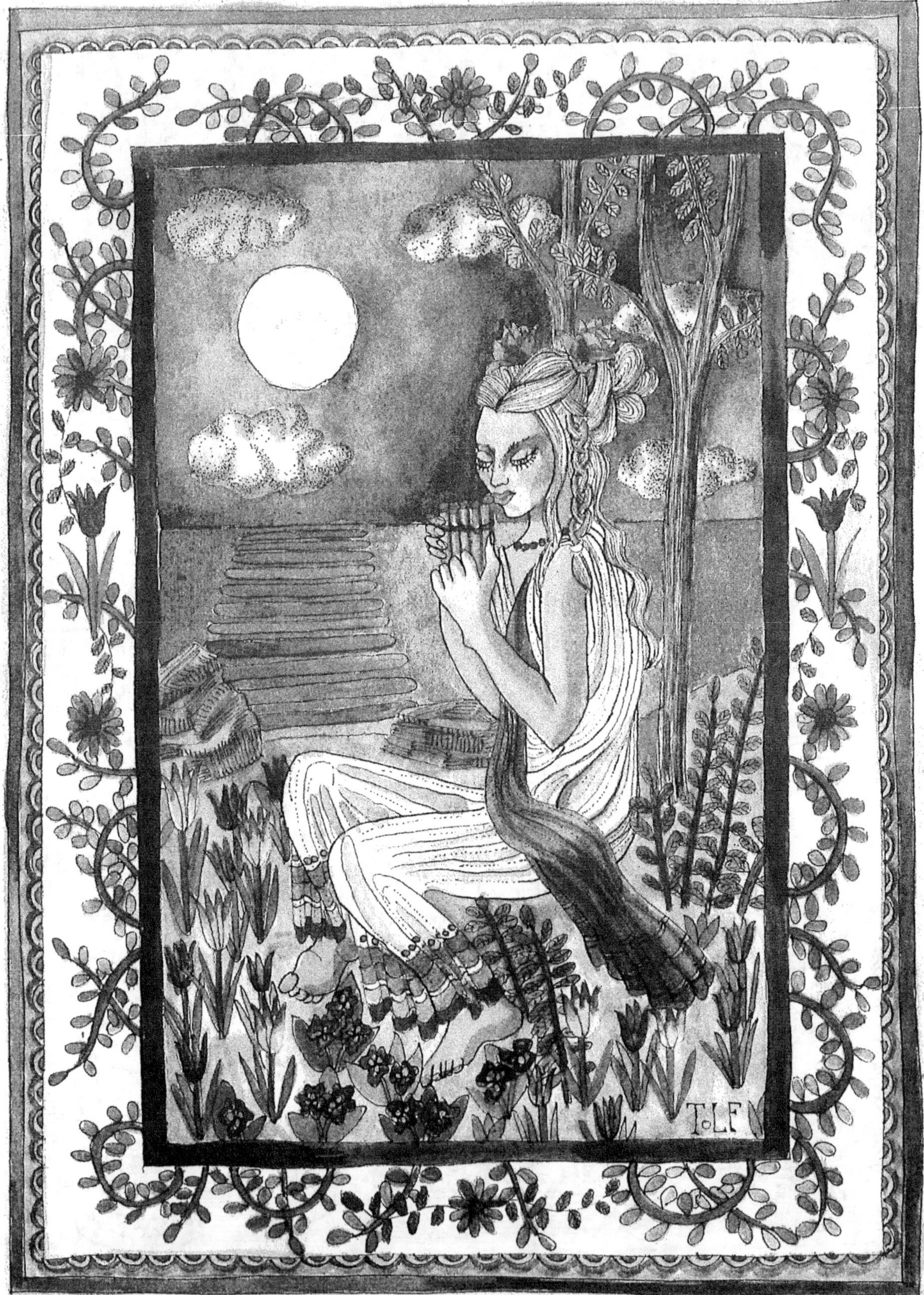

THE HERMIT

Far below the slender cliffs
where seabirds swoop like scattered ash,
twice twenty footprints from the shore
where two moons break and dolphins splash,

There lives one in a sandy cave
forever bathed in twilight's glow,
whose eyes are like the crystal gray
of ocean depths no man can know.

Upon a silver lute, she plays
the secrets of the sand and sea,
and sun-chased stars and wind-born mist
are captured in her melody.

Across a shoreline swathed in fog
where two moons rise and comets burn,
her music floats and beckons one
whose soul can hear, whose heart can learn.

Within a crevice carved by time,
below the cliffs, beyond the spin
of fortune's wheel, she plays her song,
and waits for one to come within.

WHEN MISHA SLEEPS

When Misha sleeps, he's like a shell,
all swirled around and sealed up tight.
His tail is tucked beneath his chin,
toes touch a nose that's silky night.

I hold a seashell to my ear
and hear the ocean's roar and hiss.
I nuzzle into Misha's fur:
oh, hear the rumble of his bliss!

CLAIRE PLAYING BRAHMS

Beauty is a Janus,
and life is her domain.
Like Latin god, she bears two faces—
one is joy, and one is pain.

I saw a pack of bandit crows
ascending in a cluster tight—
in frenzy to attain the sky,
they screamed and flapped with all their might

Till suddenly the great wind chose
to let the creatures ride his back.
They swooped and scattered easily
as ashes—feather specks of black.

Seeing how those frantic wings
in hovering commotion,
were poured across the morning sky
was beauty; it was joy in motion.

*

Music floats beyond her room.
Gently now, the keys unroll
an aching, tender melody
that twists and wrenches at my soul.

Sweet notes touch human suffering,
forgotten dreams that millions had.
Please stop! I can no longer listen.
It is too lovely … and too sad.

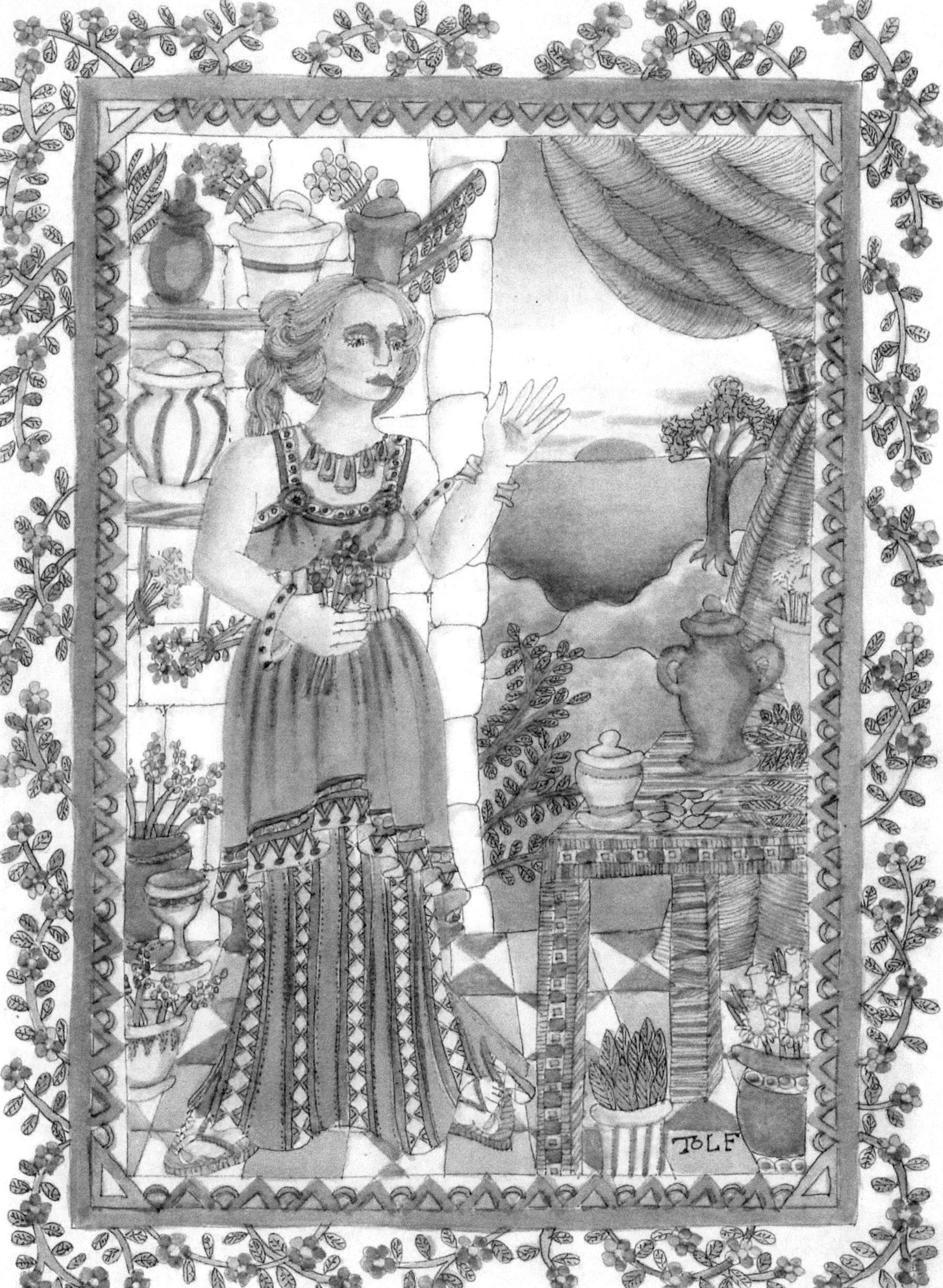
TOLF

THE PRIVATE, QUIET DREAMS

What happens to the private, quiet dreams
of modest men who die and are forgotten,
but never lived to see their hopes fulfilled?
Have *they* died, too? Are they decayed and rotten
and food for worms, or do dreams haunt the earth
like homeless children wandering indifferent streets
until an artist gathers them in song?
Is that what makes some melodies so sweet?
When night falls and the light of living dims,
what happens to the private, quiet dreams.

FIREFLIES

I've heard world-weary students say
existence is a bore, for they
have read the weighty texts of those
dismissing life in brilliant prose.
I think they're wrong. I've had my share
of serious angst, but write this where
blue gardens under velvet skies
are lit with golden fireflies.
Maybe we *don't* deserve our fate—
this transient vale of tears—but wait!
a fickle star now bright and calm
just landed in my open palm.

SEALS

I think that God
did a very good job

making magpies and mares
and brown spectacled bears,

and giraffes and Great Danes
and Rumanian cranes

and flamingos and eels—
but especially seals.

Did you ever observe
the fine motion and curve

of a seal swimming round
some blue sea nook or pond?

He's as languorous and slow
as a mermaid, you know,

with the same liquid grace,
but a puppy dog's face!

But oh, when they clamber
up rocks, where's the glamour?

They wriggle and wrangle
like trout in a tangle,

and when with a grunt,
they've the view that they want,

boast their feat to the sky
or a gull going by,

and then *that* being done,
flop to sleep in the sun.

Just last week at the zoo
(maybe *you* were there too)

when I should have been mopping
or grocery shopping,

I spent half the day
watching seals bark and play.

One climbed to the edge
of the pool's rocky ledge

and lay staring and blinking,
his long whiskers twinkling,

all shining and black.
We blinked and stared back.

He seemed curious—quite!—
but extremely polite,

accepting our praise
with a bright solemn gaze,

and when he was quite through,
with no further ado

(but an admirable cool)
flipped back into the pool.

The crowd drifted, was gone,
but I stayed on and on

as the seals floated by,
eyelids closed to the sky,

blissful critters at sea,
happy simply to be.

WHITE HORSE IN GREEN DUSK

Inspired by a painting by Herman Menzel

A white horse sleeps alone at dusk
as light winds dip to lift his mane
and stroke his face. In perfect trust,
a white horse sleeps. No fear will stain

the sweet, cold brook and fragrant grass
he dreams of on his darkening hill.
No hurt, no harm will mar this place.
He sleeps in peace and always will.

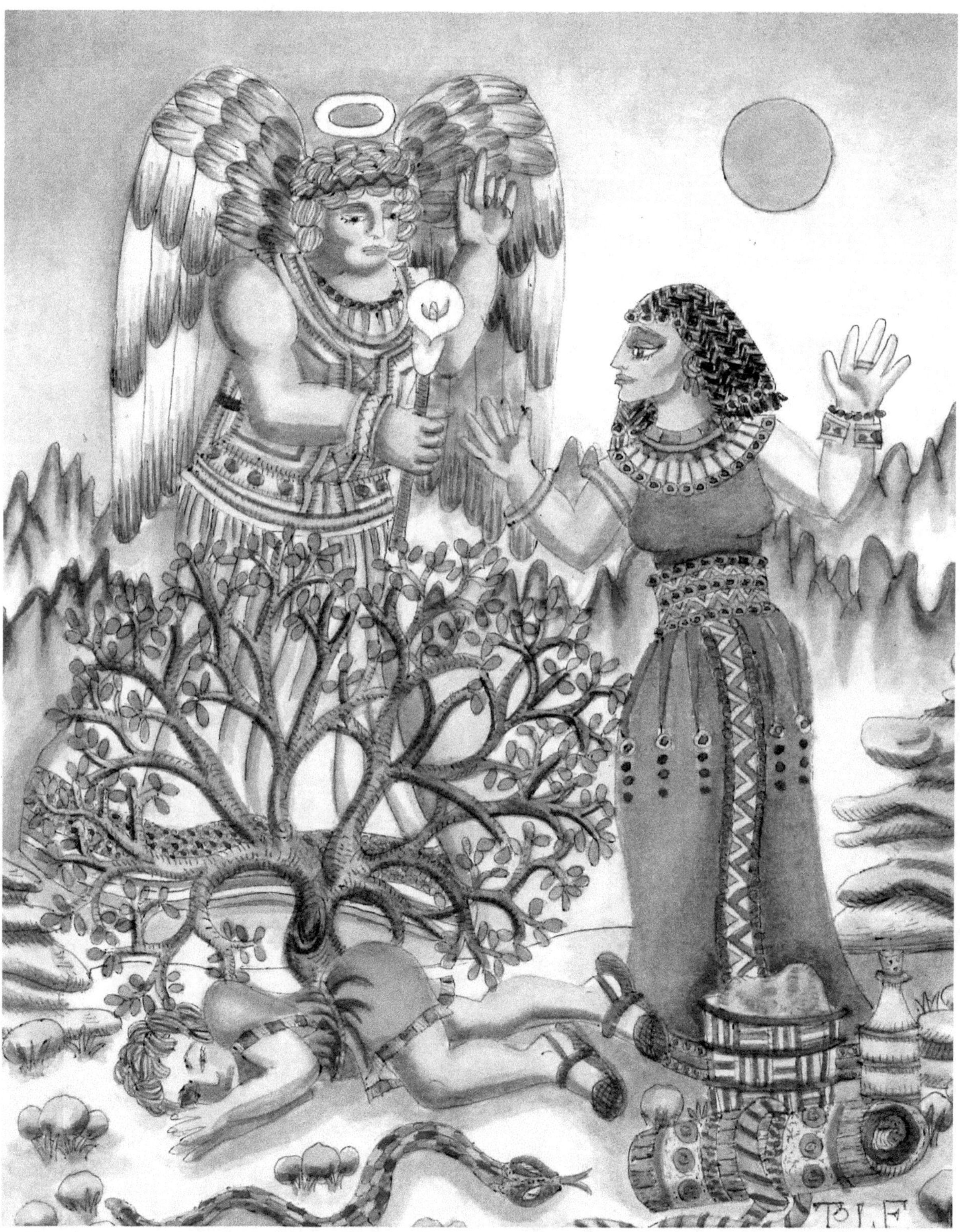

THE ISLAND OF DISCUSSION

An island in Scotland, where in the past those with arguments traveled to sort out their problems

Let's sail to the Isle of Discussion,
unpack ancient grievances there.
Good whiskey we'll sip, and sweet honey cakes munch
under fir trees in lake-scented air.

They say time on this mossy-green island
heals grudges and mends cruel wounds.
It might be the meadows, it might be the mist,
but sworn enemies leave its shore friends.

Let's sail to the Isle of Discussion,
for I hurt you, and you hurt me.
Let's talk and let's listen in lake-scented air
that mingles with birdsong, then drifts to the sea.

FRAGMENT

Let me be with you
for just an hour
tomorrow, and from time to time—
an hour, no more.

That little is enough
to pull from me
the need to better all I am,
the ache to be

as you imagine me—
or as you might,
or as I tell myself you do
in secret thought,

For we were never friends.
We are not now,
but meet, and talk, and do not touch—
nor could you know,

You being kind but far,
and I polite,
the fire and hope you wake in me,
nor guess how bright

my soul, my life becomes
from thought of you,
as if my consciousness were cleft
and light broke through

and followed to my heart,
giving, like grace,
a reason for its beating still,
a thankfulness.

THE WILD BEASTS

He was with the wild beasts and the angels looked after him. Mark: 1:13

Honey and locust, rock and sun.
The soft eyes of a desert hare.
She trembles, edges closer still,
and lets him stroke a silken ear.

Shadow and starlight, cave and wind.
A lion sleeps beside a man.
The night is cold, their breath one cloud.
The man cries out—and wakes alone.

GOBLIN FRUIT

In purple dusk, bare trees are thick
with juicy blackbirds—goblin fruit!—
studding the limbs of three great elms
in deep December—cold-eyed, mute.

All day they laced the sky with caws
enraged and brassy, raw as fright.
Now wordlessly they watch men pass
as twilight ripens into night.

HAPPINESS

Quicksilver sifting, shifting river-swift,
or crystals glazed and glittering on snow
where shade and sunlight play, are like the gift
of happiness impulsive gods bestow.
Dropped from the clouds, a sudden golden shower
of joy—then like the swift-dissolving dawn
or fragile bloom and fold of desert flower,
the rainbow rush of happiness is gone,
and all is gray. The momentary sun
is snatched away by jealous gods again,
and those who wake in shadow linger on
bemused, with longing arms outstretched in vain.
And wonder what they did to earn that glow
of bliss—and what they did to make it go.

LILLYBIRD, THE ENLIGHTENED CAT

Lillybird's a sunny cat
with golden fur and golden eyes.
Her body sings of cheetah grace,
of tawny plains and golden skies.

I found her on a dumpster top,
and bless the day our gazes met.
We formed a circle then and there.
My Lilly's an Enlightened Cat.

She's brave and sweet and smart and knows
I can't compare, yet daily, she
regards me with pure Buddha love
and thumps her tail approvingly.

CHILDREN OF THE DAY

The world is not romantic; humans are.
And children of the day who drink the sky,
and ride the racing clouds and feel a star
set fire in their own hearts, are bound to cry

that all that makes their souls clap with delight—
a diving bird, a slice of yellow sun,
the best of man and nature, dark and light—
is truth, for truth and beauty are as one.

Or so a poet famously declared,
Appearing to ignore a side of truth
unblessed by love, or nightingales, or youth.

Yet this man's heart had tasted black despair.
He alchemized that suffering into song.
So who am I to say that he is wrong.

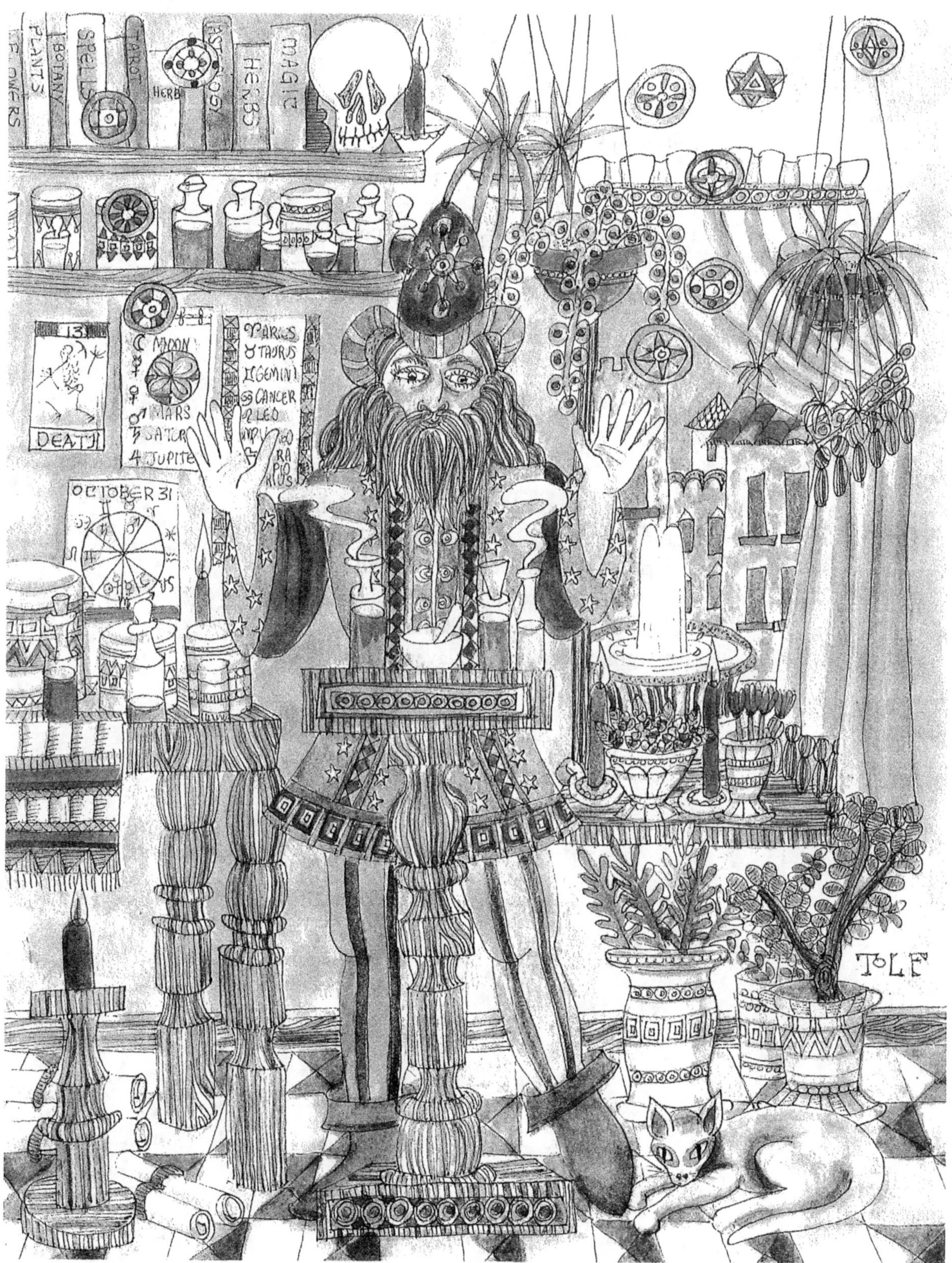

PLANTS
BOTANY
SPELLS
TAROT
HERB
HERBS
MAGIC
13
DEATH
MOON
MARS
ARIES
TAURUS
GEMINI
CANCER
LEO
OCTOBER 31
TOLF

SUMMER NIGHT, LISTENING TO DEBUSSY

To take a tree—a star—a face—a grief—
transform it into breathing stone or page
or swirling blues and greens that dance and rage;
to take remembered love or one red leaf
and pour it onto canvas, into word,
is magical, yet magic I understand.
But this ... these sounds ... how could a man have *heard*
the beauty of a young girl or the wind?

How could he conjure music from a child,
or form a flowing cadence out of light?
Creation baffles mind! Yet I am filled
with what he once conceived, hearing tonight
each fiber of a simple piece he wrote
that seems to probe life's layers and to hold,
within austerity of space and note,
the sweetness and the sorrow of the world.

"HOW STILL THE RIDDLE LIES"

—Emily Dickinson

Under snowbank, sleeps a flower.
Deep in flower, dreams a fruit.
In this fruit glows sun and harvest.
Nesting deeper: frost and root.

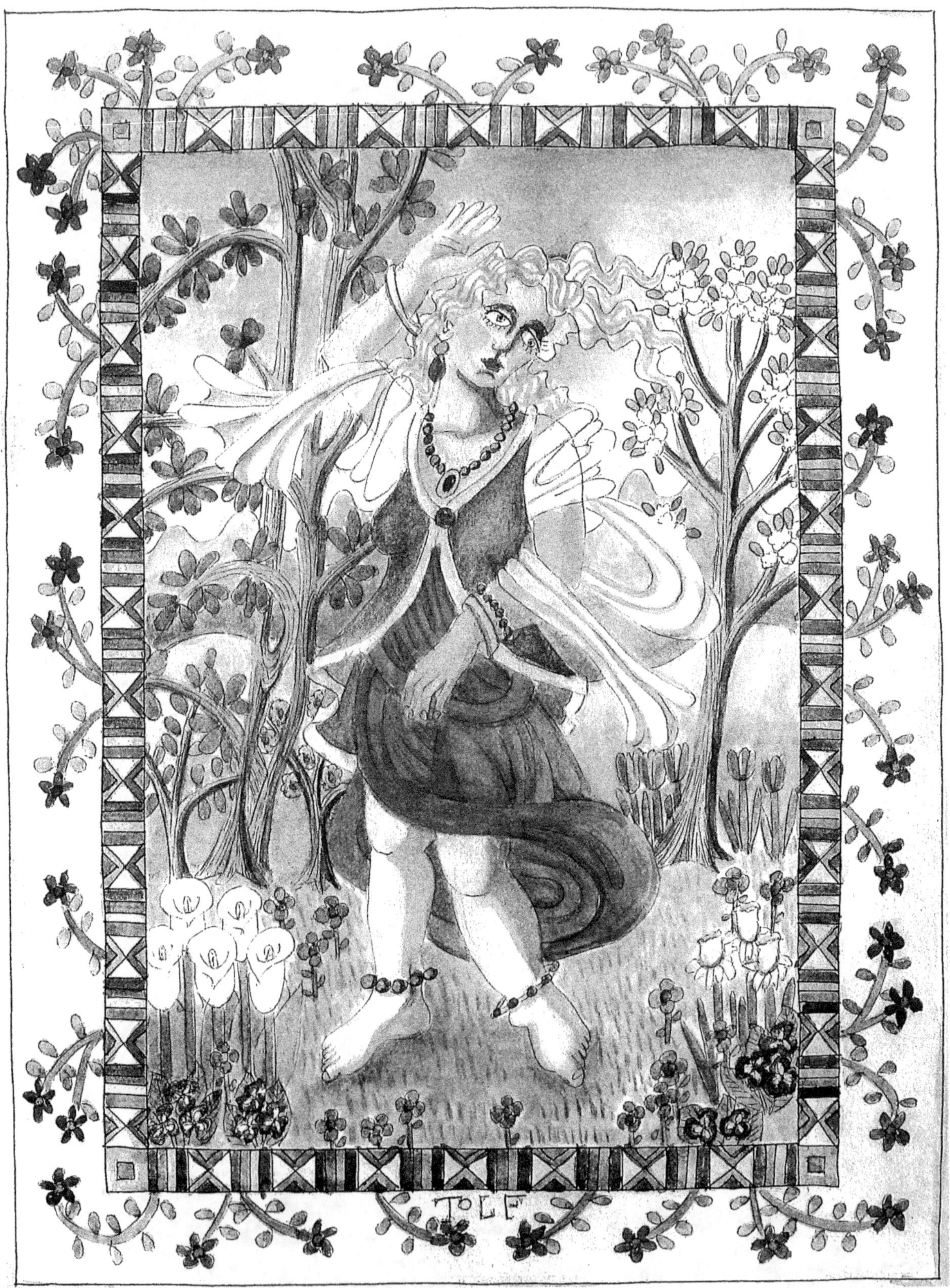
TOLF

THIS NIGHT'S A WITCH

This night's a witch. She's drunk me full of darkness
and conjured wizard notions in my mind.
Black shadows drift like shades of roaming memories;
dark leaves seem stirred by wandering dreams, not wind.

Tall branches bend like ancients sharing secrets
long kept: and high above me, ringed in haze,
Moon seems a mask that knows more than she's telling,
hiding her knowledge in a cloudy gaze.

AFTER READING THE BOOK OF JOB

The thunder god who wrapped himself in wind
and rode a howling tempest to the earth
to answer Job's lament, could merely blind
that servant with the brilliance of his work,
but could not give Job reason for the pain
he suffered. And how could he when this song
of man in sorrow flowed from heart of man?
How could a trembling soul and mortal tongue
conceive divine reply? Man could but sing
in poetry as beautiful as light
of how the seas were chained and stars were hung
by One who had created sun and night
and all that turned to dust. Man could but boast
the glory of a god whose very splendor
shamed cowering Job from asking what was just.
Man could but praise a god who gave no answer.

THE COTTONWOOD TREE

As if I were a holy man
who *had* the sacred right to hear
the murmurous chant of a great tree
stirred white-leafed in the morning air,

just so I hear the cottonwood
outside my room—my constant friend—
with eyelids closed, am borne upon
a sea-like rise and fall of sound,

becoming healed. I dreamt of trees
last night. They swayed and barred the sky
like graceful dancers, slim and brown.
I woke at 2:00 a.m. to spy,

illicitly, a large white jewel
entangled in black leaves outside
that was a moon. (Four ghostly walls
washed pale by silver testified

that moonlight still exists, though mostly
swallowed by electric streets.)
I will not tell you why I wept;
some secrets we were meant to keep.

I'll only say it's morning now,
and in young light, I understand
a little more that thing called grace,
for sweet as chimes in summer wind,

my cottonwood is lulling me
as if I were her only child.
I listen to her loveliness,
remembering hope. Becoming healed.

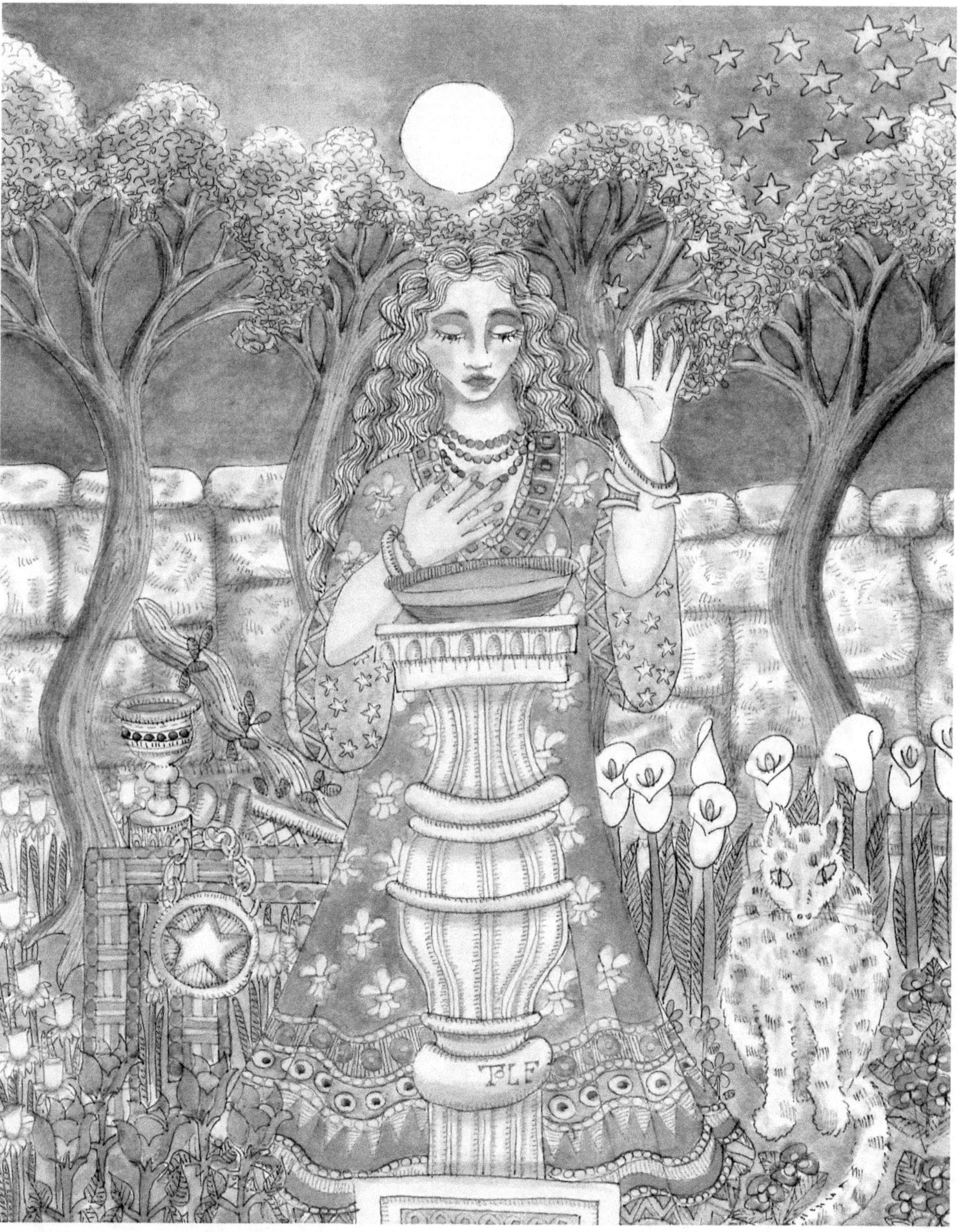

THE MOON-FLOWER

Moon carols in a gypsy's veins,
and swells the sea from shore to shore.
Moon rides the panther's eye at night,
and charms a shining flower to stir

long after other flowers fold—
to stir and open silver-white,
slim petal-arms stretched toward the stars,
swaying and sighing with delight.

She and the moon are dearest friends.
Each night they whisper secrets sweet.
Moon-flower drinks the white moon's milk,
then, drunk with beauty, goes to sleep.

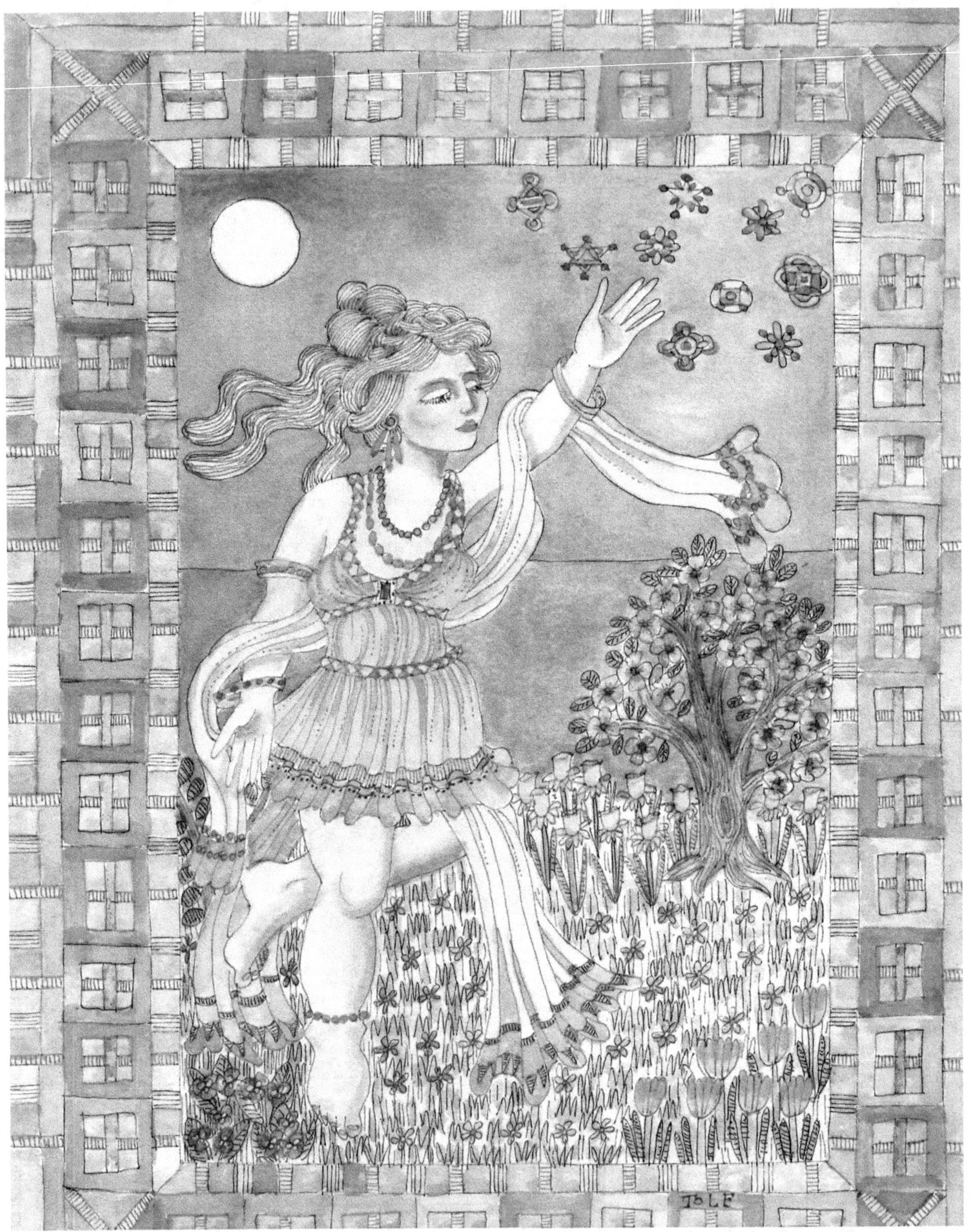

ALL LIVING THINGS

Summer's leaf-green thickets led
to clustered oak leaves, crimson red.
In transient glory, they remain,
till raked by wind and swept by rain,
they form a soggy bed to meet
the heels of restless creatures feet.
All things in time are claimed by earth,
who from them mixes magic birth.
Through her, eternal spring is bred,
and bluebells burst from April mud.

FAREWELL

You've wandered through a wood of poems.
I hope they gave you some delight—
The hermit, moon and marigolds,
the seals and Clee, the rainy night.
It's been a checkered journey, mixed
with joy and strangeness, dark and bright.

"Everything that lives is holy,"
so said Blake and so say I,
and swear the heart's a mystery
older than time, deeper than sky.
I dipped a pen into my heart,
wrote songs that laugh and rhymes that cry.

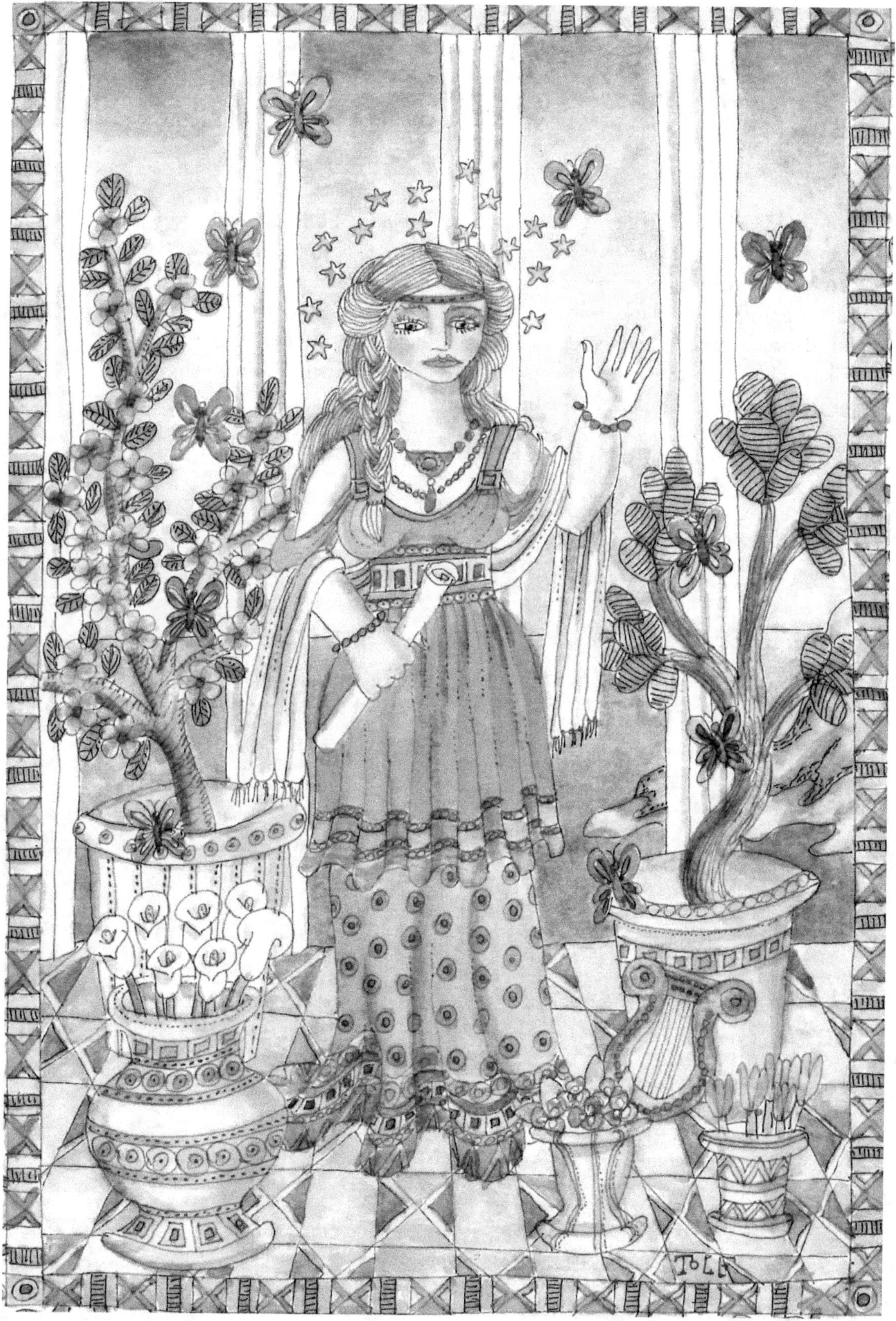
ToLE

ABOUT THE AUTHOR

Francine Marie Tolf's poems and essays have been published widely in journals such as *Southern Humanities Review, Poetry East, Contrary Magazine, Rattle,* and *Water~Stone Review*. She has received two Minnesota State Arts Board Grants as well as grants from the Elizabeth George Foundation and the Barbara Deming Foundation. Francine lives and works in Minneapolis, where she loves taking long walks around the city's beautiful lakes and the Mississippi River. She shares an apartment with her golden cat, Lilly.

ABOUT THE ARTIST

Gale Tolf was an award winning artist, writer, and teacher with a Masters in Gifted Education. Her solo art exhibits include *Harlequinade*, Mandala Gallery, Pacific Grove, CA; *Women and Roses*, Carl Cherry Foundation, Carmel, CA; *Myths*, Northeastern Illinois University; *Day of the Dead*, Café Express, Evanston, IL; and *Midwest Mythology*, Bicentennial Theater, Joliet, IL. Gale participated in group exhibits held in Chicago (School of the Art Institute, Swedish Art Museum in Chicago, Artemisia Gallery, NAME Gallery, and Objects Gallery) and the Monterey area (Pacific Grove Museum, Monterey Public Library, and Monterey Museum of Art). Gale's illustrations have been published widely in literary journals.

For inspiration and subject matter, Gale drew deeply from myths, fairytales, poetry, and the Bible. She was a voracious reader whose favorite authors included Carl Jung, Walt Whitman, Rainer Maria Rilke, and Shakespeare. She once noted that The Bard was one of her best friends: "He knew more about psychology than Freud and had a sense of humor to boot!"

Gale suffered from bipolar disorder. She felt great compassion for anyone dealing with mental illness. These words are from one of the many poetry collections she self-published:

"The next time you see someone suffering from mental illness—perhaps a bag lady muttering to herself and looking godawful—don't avert your eyes. Look her in the eye and talk to her. Inside is a person who wants everything out of life—just like you do. And that person is a warrior. Maybe a wounded warrior, but a warrior just the same. Because inside that human being is an intricate, exquisite mind and a loving benevolent heart—in camouflage—but there."

www.ingramcontent.com/pod-product-compliance
Lightning Source LLC
LaVergne TN
LVHW080921110826
845155LV00039B/122
* 9 7 8 1 9 3 6 6 7 1 4 8 9 *